Life Behind Bars

Stories and Encounters

Book Two

Kyle Branche

DEDICATION

To all the bars I've ever worked in, all the private parties and events I've ever worked at, all the bartenders, barbacks, waiters, cocktail waitresses, busboys, dishwashers, cooks, chefs, managers, GM's, owners and brands I've ever worked with, all the liquor reps and spirit houses, and to all the magazines, editors and publishers I've ever written articles, columns and feature cover stories for. You have been the grist for my mill for 30 years.

CONTENTS

Note: I wrote all the stories in a random mode, no chronological order of occurrence, and I've kept them that way in this book. All of the stories listed and lined up above are in the exact order in which I wrote them. Therefore, it allows the reader to pick or select at their choosing what story they prefer to read at any given time, or they can simply be read in the order here.

ACKNOWLEDGMENTS

Special thanks to bartender/friend Kellie Nicholson for her support and techs-pertise with editing and formatting on how to do this and how to do that while still keeping within an artistic vision, look and style of one's own. Much appreciated!

Special thanks to my friend Martin Veider for all things computer-related, as I would have never made it this far without your continued faith and patience, and excellence in keeping my words and hard drive alive in the online world while my education never ends.

To view a more visual experience with the stories beyond the capabilities with words alone, there are pictures and videos that coincide with many of the stories in this book located on my Blog, where the stories originated – LABartender.wordpress.com.

Website: KylesCocktailHotel.com

1

NIGHTS AT PROVENCE

In 1998, I was mildly searching around for another place of bar work. Café Bellissimo, where I played bar manager and bartender, was leveling off its hectic business volume over a long stretch of time after four years of popularity in the surrounding communities of Thousand Oaks, north on the 101 about 16 miles from where I live.

Of course, it didn't help that the menu prices must've raised two or three times in the last year, for reasons unknown to us, scratching our heads over it, and noticing a drop in the normal business we were used to on certain nights of the week. I keep aware of signals for no more reason than to escape before any potential cave-in.

I had often talked with the owner's girlfriend when she sat at the bar, and one day she mentioned a place she had recently heard was looking for a bar/nightclub manager over in Westlake Village just off the 101, and a few miles closer to home. It was the resort hotel and golf course property, The Westlake Village Inn. A few days later, I went to check it out after making the proper calls in to verify the position was still open.

When I arrived, my contact was a lady named Sherry. We met and had about a half-an-hour interview, and she offered me the position. I accepted and gave my two weeks notice to Café B. They were in a quick need to replace, as from what I heard, the previous bar manager had to go away for six months or more following his second DUI, which may have included causing an accident with injury, or something of that nature. I didn't quite get the specifics on the issue, but didn't ask for them either. He was a nice enough guy when I met him, as he showed me around and hung at the club for a few nights over the weekend before he left.

A beautiful 17-acre property on Agoura Road with Mediterranean-designed grounds, where Old Mulholland Highway is just a short drive up into the Santa Monica Mountains, it has The Villa, eight categories of rooms and suites, a golf course, a restaurant (Mediterraneo), tennis courts, banquet facilities, a gazebo for weddings, an acre-sized working vineyard with 550 vines, an herb and vegetable garden, and the nightclub called Provence (now Bogie's Lounge), that I was in charge of.

There were 12 staff at the bar – bartenders, cocktail waitresses, barbacks, and security. This was the beginning of fifty-hour work weeks for me. It was a temporary position, so I did it for the experience, and as a safe bridge out of Café B. Not my favorite level of burn time on the clock, but I knew I could get some other side work done while floating about. I'm a bit too motivated creatively to become as loungy as this position could afford me.

The club itself was a great space, with the classic long bar built for two and a back, wood floors, and an outside half-moon patio bar that serviced a U-shaped wrap-around that overlooked a Japanese Koi pond, with the golf course just across the water. There is a lot of money out in this area, so it was their party and dance club, a close-by home away from home. We had a different band in each week on Thursday through Saturday nights, and I, after the first month or so, became responsible for booking them in from a talent agency a month to six weeks in advance.

This was my fifth or sixth bar/club to manage in my F&B journey, so I was used to the basic procedures, but here I didn't have to tend bar except in a case of emergency, where coming out of Café B, I did both, like I've done before elsewhere. I had a great crew for a staff, whom many had been there for quite some time. Effectively, my job was just to continue the ship on course. Easy enough!

To a degree, we were like the untouchables. The collective experience of all of us was hard to beat. One particular cocktail waitress on the staff, Jeannie, had been there as long as the original owner, somewhere between 30-40 years. She told me one day that she said to him "When you retire, John, then I'll retire". She was a classic on the floor, and knew every inch of the property. You could count on her like a sundial.

We had Paul behind the bar, who had been there for over ten years, but also worked the wood during the weeknights at the restaurant, Tuscany, just down the street. Working the bar alongside Paul on weekends was J.B., who was the original 1988 Flair Bartending Grand Champion, when he worked at Fridays. Another bartender named John worked the bar during the weeknights, so we would hang out, and both Chrissy and John would share the weekend shifts out in the patio bar. Then we had our barback, Manny the crazy Columbian, who had been on the bar staff for umpteen years as well. And with Jimmy as one of our four long-tenured security and door guys, all areas of the club were covered from back to front. So as you can see, they had the train. I was just riding in coach.

The shirt and tie was something I was used to, but I wore a vest instead of a coat in the weekly management meetings. Not an act of defiance, it was simply lighter and more comfortable in summer weather. It was nice to have the option instead of it being a strict requirement. The bar was a different animal, and whether they knew it or not, so was I. I adhere in many respects to the position and job description, but I'm no stepford conformist to the marching powder of management, not if it limits the capabilities of why they hired me.

With me, as a manager, I operated loosely-tight with the staff. There's something to be said for when nothing needs to be said! I think we may have had one initial meet, conveniently on a busy weekend night when everyone was about to start shift, but after that, if I had updates, changes, notifications, corrections, or anything to say, I would type it all up on a one or two-pager, and make copies for each of them, including security. No need to have a dozen staff members get on the road during off-shift hours just for an unnecessary hour-long face-to-face. Some had day jobs or school, therefore impossible to get everyone together at a mid-to-late afternoon time, anyway. Forget it!

I don't play the power trip role like some diehards in suits, not with my tribe. My role was to make my staff look good and get them what they needed. Their role was to make me look good, if they wanted me around. So in effect, all of us managed the club, and took care of each other. But I was the sucker who had to go to the 2:00 pm weekly department head meetings!

Sometime during the second week on the job, I met John Notter, the owner. He peeked in the office real quick while I was at my desk. This was at a time where Salsa dancing had become popular, shortly after the years when country-western line-dancing became so big. He mentioned that he'd like me to create an evening during the week, either Tuesday or Wednesday, to have a Salsa night with dance lessons. He was in luck, as I just happened to know a married couple who taught. They agreed to do it, and a few weeks later we had it going. We were supposed to have weekly radio blasts to get the word out, but something fizzled out with that after a couple weeks. I disagreed with having a cover charge for this night, but I was overruled. The dance instructors had to be paid, the Salsa DJ, radio too, so justification had to be covered. Though it was somewhat a minimal charge, which isn't a bother to the affluent residents in the neighborhood, it still didn't take off in the way any of us had hoped. Unfortunate, as the room was good for it.

I created a club entertainment hotline where I voiced the message of events and the bands of each week. A couple three weeks after the Salsa night ended, I filled the spot with an original idea of my own. I put together an Art night, making contact with the College and the Chamber of Commerce, until I got a hold of an Artist's Association in the nearby area. For the elegance of the property and the beauty of the bar's main room, it was a perfect fit for a nice 5-8 pm event for established artists in the community. We had a different artist come in each week and set-up their paintings on canvas. There was no cover charge. It was also a more flexible fit when it came to the guests staying in rooms overnight or longer, as they could stop by for some cheese and crackers, maybe a glass of wine, enjoy the works of an area artist for a while, see a painting they may be interested in, then a quick walk over to the restaurant for dinner.

However, I had to make the hours of display worth it for the artists to take the time, as they were the ones who had to load all their canvas and easels into a van or truck, unload and set-up in the bar's floor space, load back up at the end, and then unload again back home. That's a lot of schlepping for the possibility of no sales during an exhibit. But creating a space for it was worth a shot, and for the artist, you never know who's going to be walking in the door to view the work. With the clientele that stayed at the hotel, all it takes is the recognition of one person.

The weekly management meetings helped me get to know other department heads on the property, which was a good thing considering my hours were opposite of just about everyone else's. There was about a dozen of us at the long table. I got to know the Executive Chef and the Banquet Manager pretty well, as their offices were closer by. One of those get-togethers we held in the bar one afternoon, and for the occasion, a couple nights before I went into the main kitchen/galley and prepared my popular

Sangria recipe in large batch, and served it up as an afternoon beverage. With plenty left over, I took it to the bar and we served it as a house specialty until it ran out.

The G.M. and I got along pretty well, but rarely spoke or saw each other. One time in passing through a banquet area, she kissed me on the lips, and we started talking about my work for a couple minutes, and that I was doing a good job. That was nice of her, as she was cool, but the kiss was a little unexpected, though no complaints from me! She was a beauty, and in this type of work environment, you hear all kinds of rumors on the property. I wanted nothing to do with being in the middle of anything. The drama some people create is amazing. One meeting I was in, it was the birthday of someone in the room. A kiss on the lips took place between two people. I thought that was kind of weird, maybe I just hadn't been around long enough. Some others were looking around the room, though, so I knew I wasn't alone. But hey, kissing is okay . . .

I had to watch out for the banquet department on occasion, during some of the busy season, as their rooms available for events weren't always of the size they needed for guest counts, and they weren't about to turn down an event for that reason, so at times they would rent out the nightclub bar and patio area to accompany their needs. It's one thing if it happens during the week, but a Friday or Saturday evening, most of my staff and the regular club-goers in the area wouldn't get much notice at all. We had huge crowds on the weekends, so someone would have to be at the door to turn away our normal business, and the band would have to be notified of a cancellation. The problem with this "allowed" override of that department into mine is it doesn't take but just a few of those occurrences too close together to make our regulars consider making somewhere else their weekend party roost. I wasn't happy seeing our numbers drop, but it was their decision, not mine. They didn't seem to need any approval!

I remember one of the banquet floor staff came to me about their gratuity issues, since they couldn't talk to Bob about it, as it seemed to be a bit, umm, questionable. One night I took a look at one of the BEO's (Banquet Event Orders) and noticed that out of the 18% gratuity charge, 10% would go to the staff, and the other 8% would go to the house, whoever that was. Management, the reason why I no longer get involved! This is even more standard practice at some hotel chains today in their banquet departments, where they now hire inexperienced "bodies" behind a bar and on the floor for events at some hourly wage of $11 or $12, but they receive none of the 18% or 20% gratuity charge. What the client holding and paying for the event doesn't know, and isn't informed of, is that the gratuity isn't going to where they think it is. They allow professional service and the direct representatives to the client and their event guests to drop in some level, in order for the suits to either make up some of their losses from a salary cut, or just take as icing on the cake, however it's sliced.

When Roger was hired as some accounting and maintenance supervisor in the office that Sherry and I shared, his nuisance abilities soon became the pain in my ass. He was trying to fit in, which was natural, but he was a little too eager to please others, feeling he had something to prove, with Sherry cheerleading team spirit I'm sure. After awhile, those two developed a bond and became a force to be reckoned with. They must've shared the same Indian name, which was "Too Much Coffee Bean Before Noon"!

Sherry would hold these banquet meetings on occasion. I would be in them. She would be going over details of upcoming events, and to try and find ways to drum up more business for their department. One of the times I pitched in the idea of having this beautiful banquet space (The Provence Room) that overlooked the water to be the spot where they can make available for a variety of touring circuit speakers of various professions and occupations to hold their talks and seminars, including famous authors, who would have loved the property, golf, and the hotel stay. Sherry looked at me like I was from another planet! It was the last time I spoke up with an idea for her potential benefit.

I just wanted to be cool, do my job, take care of the club and stay out of their way. But Roger wanted more. One particular week, he requested that him and I do the bar's liquor inventory together. That was fine, but he wanted to do it first thing in the morning, at his convenience, when he arrived for his regular 9-5 day shift. I was thinking he would be considerate enough to make it sometime between Noon and 2:00pm to work with both our schedules, as the bar didn't open until 4:00pm. No such luck. I now knew what he was up to. He was after me for something, but there was nothing to find or go after. And I don't think his actions were alone. He knew I was, and had been for years, on opposite hours. I wasn't about to play into his little game to see if I'd conform to his every need. There was nothing for Roger or Sherry to snitch on with me, so I created something for them to see how they'd run with it, and the fact that mornings are nearly impossible for me to get up, much less capable of focusing on inventory detail until sometime after Noon. I'd like to see Roger come into the bar at Midnight or 2:00am jonesing for the numerical countdown of the bottles, and everything else. "Roger, I understand those are your sleeping hours". But not mine. I'm raring to go at the witching hour.

He wanted me bright and early Monday morn (my day off), so Sunday night I brought all the bottles up and on top of the bar, sectioned and categorized to make it easier for him. He was on his own, but didn't know it yet. I slept in my usual hours. I get a phone message later that morning. He was steaming that I wasn't there ready to go. But he wasn't my boss. He went forward with it the best that he could, given the standard inventory sheets they used were anything but efficient for bar counts. He was still pissed to no end when I saw him, and that I was the one who blew his gasket made it even worse. My apology went to John, my bartender, who ended up having to put the bottles back. But I wasn't about to get up on my day off of a 50-hour week for a couple hours of something that could've easily waited until the afternoon. Roger came from a Doubletree or Hyatt hotel property, where it may have been a little more militaristic in its style at which things got done, but Westlake Inn was an independently-owned laid back property of relaxation and luxury.

The nightclub operated great for the most part. There's always a certain amount of chaos in the mix, though, like anything food and beverage, it goes with the territory, but kept to a minimum. John Notter had a good friend of his, this French guy named Eddie, who would come into the club to dance and party. He was an older guy who would make us all look bad, as he had a nasty habit of groping asses on the dance floor. The man had an ego with no shame, tried to play the European card to his advantage, while he was in with another lady! The security had told me that he'd been doing it for years, but he was Notter's buddy, so nothing could be done except to ask him to knock it off. He'd cool it for awhile, and then go right back to it, regardless of the complaints against him.

I made my own observance of it as well. I wasn't about to let this go on with the potential of losing good customers, all of us embarrassed to allow it to continue in our presence. I pulled the trigger and did something no one had ever done with Eddie. I kicked him out of the club, and had security escort him towards the door. He started giving me some lip on the way out with girl in tow, and I got right in his face about his no-consequence clause, basically telling him to get the fuck out of the club and don't come back until he can keep his hands off ass. I cared that he was Notter's buddy, but I couldn't have that shit go on any further. He took it too far and got what he deserved. Notter and I never talked about the situation when we saw each other. I'm sure he wasn't too pleased with my decision, but it's not like he could school me via policy and procedure by defending Eddie's actions, either. The situation became a draw, guns back in holster. No immunity!

Our weekends could get crazy busy. We had a lot of great bands come through and rock the house. They would be on a rotation, so we would always see them again. While I was at the helm, we broke a long-standing cover charge record on one particular night, with many other close calls. One time I took the members of the 4-piece band, Menage, over to the hotel area of the property during their break, grabbed the keys from the office, and showed them the 2-floor $750-a-night room called *The Villa*. It was pretty awesome. The lead singer was this super-nice gorgeous blonde, so I got a kick from seeing her reaction.

This lady started coming into the club on Thursday nights. Her name was Barbara. A strikingly beautiful brunette, we ended up getting introduced through another guest. One particular Thursday, we saw each other and started chatting it up, perfect weather outside, cooler near the water but balmy away. We took a stroll out and down the long walkway that led to the gazebo. Up the steps we went, alone, comfortable, and single. I had a cocktail with me and she had a glass of wine. Our slow-paced, word-teased conversation soon led to luscious wet kisses. Her sexy dress and long legs added to my weakening. I could see the heat rising in her eyes, as we kept it on the lips. I had to be careful. The heat was on me as well, and I could've been getting played. A side of the gazebo was in eye-shot of anyone who might have walked by. On the dark side, she leaned over on the railing and slowly arched her ass up in the air, her short dress no longer hiding her black G-string. My hands were all over it, and although I knew she was soaked and wanted me to take her from behind in the hardest way, I didn't know her *modus operandi* yet. In a tough decision, I felt it best to cover my own ass before I covered hers. On the hot edge of satisfying desires under the night sky, a party of four walked by on the way back to their rooms from the restaurant. Close, No cigar!

The one event I really wanted to get going was something I conceived of, called "Musicians Unhinged". With a crazy abundance of professional music talent living in the area, I wanted to get a bunch of them lined up when they weren't on tour or out of town, have them network with a few other players of their choice, book them in advance, have each individual show performed in the club, to be filmed and aired for television as a unique music series, blending musicians who've always wanted to play together in a small acoustic or semi-electric setting, but have never had the chance. Something a bit similar to what Daryl Hall (Hall & Oates) is doing today with his web show called "Live at Daryl's House".

A regular customer on the weekends owned a carpentry/woodshop business, and he was willing to build a custom stage I had designed on paper to fit the main space where the bands normally set-up for the weekends, for free, as a donation to the project.

I got to know the now legendary session and tour drummer, John "JR" Robinson, who lived in the area and frequented the club. JR is the most recorded drummer in history. I remember seeing him, a decade previous, on the Robert Palmer tour, at Irvine Meadows. He was all for it, and knew a ton of people to contact and help out. The guitarist for one of our regular and popular bands, Menage, was good friends with guitarist Steve Lukather of Toto, and Paul our bartender, when working at Tuscany, would see Richie Sambora and Heather Locklear come into the bar and hang. Paul asked Richie what he thought about the idea and if he'd be interested, and he said yes. This was just the beginning stages. Others who lived in the area were Eddie Money, Rickee Lee Jones, percussionist Paulinho de Costa, Gino Vanneli, Frankie Valli, Richard Carpenter, Alex Van Halen, Neil Diamond, and Brad Wilk (drummer for Rage), to name a few. It's too bad I was 4-5 years late on arriving at the Westlake Inn, as he had passed away in 1994, but Harry Nilsson lived just over in Agoura Hills at the time.

Malibu was just a 20-minute drive from PCH through the canyon on Kanan Road over to the club, so all those musicians living closer to the beach, though up in the hills, were still in shouting distance to be included as well. My goal was to put an 8-12 show season together that would be shot from the last six weeks of Summer and through the first six weeks of Fall, kissing two seasons for different energies in the air, from an audience perspective, and for the musicians. Our regular club-goers, who were more 40-somethings, though still covered a wide age range, would have loved it. It was right up their affluent alley. We probably would have shot the "Live" performances on Sunday or Monday evenings.

Unfortunately, this was towards the end of my short reign. I should have talked with Notter about the idea, but he wasn't always around or available, and to jump over other management ranks would have got me in more hot water, when it was already starting to boil. Though, if I'd seen him I would have, and took the heat for good cause and intention, as something told me not to tell the other Dept. heads. The idea was just too good to be screwed up by someone else, if they would have taken it and ran. Though Notter and one other executive office at their other property back east that I spoke with occasionally, wanted me to create ideas and events for the room and the community, there were others on the Westlake property that worked against my success. I was caught in the middle.

One of my staff at the time, when I felt my end coming near, had caught me for a moment in the parking lot when I was grabbing something from my truck. He let me know that management had asked him to temporarily replace me until they could find a full-time new guy to take over. He declined, primarily out of respect for me, but also because he couldn't pull the extra hours and didn't want to get involved. My crew was good to me, and I was good to them. Like I said before, we had each other's backs. With this hospitality-version of *Peyton Place*, we needed to.

A couple weeks later, I got the word from my peep on the inside that the new guy was sitting at a table in the club with a friend on a Friday night. I couldn't help but walk by a couple times and try to look him in the eye, mildly letting him know that I knew. He was having a difficult time reciprocating. It was okay, though. I was ready to go at that point, but they were going to have to let me go. I wasn't going to walk on my own, giving them ease and satisfaction. I didn't want me gone, they did.

They finally made the move one afternoon after I arrived for my shift. Sherry asked me to come with her to the main office, so I hesitated over some paperwork, then followed slowly, which seemed to irritate her more, acting like I didn't know, when it was them who leaked it all over the property. It was nice to know that many who worked at the Inn would miss me, but Sherry couldn't deal with me anymore. As she was marching ahead of me down the covered walkway about ten paces in her stride, I just looked at her and shook my head. We get to the office, and Chris and Sherry gave the standard reason "We're going in a different direction". I got paid off with final checks, vacation, and bonus/profit share, and I was done.

Sometime after I had left, I was still getting calls about the continued shit going on, with the big new rumor that the devil's husband had been fired from a nearby country club on embezzlement allegations. Whether they were true or not, who knows, but I heard they had both soon skipped town and moved to another state. She loses her job and gains a bad reputation by spousal action. Karma, two birds with one stone.

What nobody knew about me on the property was this. Just a matter of months before the Westlake gig, still at Café B, I ended up in the hospital with a life and death emergency that stemmed from an emergency surgery just a couple years prior, in the summer of 95'. A blockage in my body, from scar tissue or whatever, had pretty much shut down my system. I was losing fluids dramatically over many days and couldn't consume anything. I was down for the count, and I knew it. My brain was taking me on that short film of my entire life that you hear about. I wasn't a stranger to near-death experiences. This was Number 5, dating all the way back to childhood.

Finally admitted in, the doctors didn't know what was wrong, and after a week of IV, never really found out. I had lost so much weight from inability to consume food or drink, the only thing I had left to hold onto was just enough energy for the attention on every breath while lying lifeless in the hospital bed. I also hadn't slept in seven days. Total body deprivation. Something had intervened outside of me or any person. My body reversed itself from its wrong direction after a dream I had where I was flying across an endless desert plain below, but elsewhere, not here. It was a desert of dwellers.

Surviving this ordeal of illness took a while to get through. After I got out of the hospital, for the following year's period of time or more, I was floating slowly between two different planes of existence, back and forth, even when I was driving. Nothing mattered anymore. No worries, no crisis, no concerns. It was the greatest feeling of complete freedom and disappearance that I've ever had. This was all happening at the time I was at the Westlake Village Inn. It was taking this long to fully get back into my body, and I wasn't complaining, wishing it would have lasted longer, forever. I had surrendered everything, and left it to the heavens for guidance until I could ride the horse again, or cared to!

It's why I was still a little thin and not at my ideal body weight when I arrived. Above all, it was the complete reason why almost anything and everything that went on there during my time would just fall off my shoulders, laughing inside at something that would bother the normal person enough to feel compelled to engage. Well, except for the "Eddie" moment! That was a legitimate call. I won the battle but lost the war!! This was also when I started seeing things before they occurred, knowing things in advance, and reading/listening to others before they spoke. After Westlake, when I wanted or needed work, the phone would ring. This altered state of consciousness slowly put me back on track, energetically, for the earth plane once again. For what, I don't know. I was so much better . . . off! Since then, I've had a Number 6 . . .

2

TEMPLE OF THE DOGG

It was the Summer of 2006, with hot temperatures in the city. I get a call from the guys at Bar One Catering to work a special one-off event that was happening in downtown Los Angeles at an old historic church around second street, maybe third. A fundraiser of sorts, there would be about a thousand people in attendance. The concert – Snoop Dogg. Though Bar One had on staff close to twenty people overall for the show, Jeffrey and I had the most experience, so we were always put in any hot spots of bar activity. Aaron needed one more, so I brought my friend Kelly with me, a past manager from Café Bellissimo in Woodland Hills, where I use to work in 1994.

She lives nearby, so we drove down together in my truck. Thankfully, there was a huge parking lot just the next block down from the church. We entered the house of the holy through the open side door, where many others were going in and out. Meeting up with Aaron and his assistant, Kelly would fill one of the bar stations on the main floor with several others, tables set up in a big square. I find out I'm the sole bartender to work the VIP bar, positioned just to the left of the main stage. Cool ! Jeffrey had the other VIP bar located on a riser further out in the main floor. Both areas were roped off with security.

I was ready and rockin' to perform at high speed on my own, with my trusted barback nearby. Working solo is nice sometimes. You can set-up your own *mise en space* for efficient moves and volume depending on what type of bar you have to work with, of which you never know until you get there. Is there enough room for product, tool, and ice placement? Is it not enough? Can we modify this? Can we change that? Preparation is always the key to smooth running at a bar.

I was made aware that my section had approximately 60-80 invited passes. With this event, my guess was most of them would show up. It was roomy enough for a comfortable number, designed as a sizeable sofa lounge, with small cocktail tables against the wall, and plenty of stand-up ground. I was curious as to who was invited and who would hang out in the area.

With a little time to spare, I took my shirt with me and went outside to dress and have a quick smoke, down the sidewalk and in between the street and where the two tour buses were parked. It was finally starting to cool down outside. This is the time of year where the sun doesn't set until 7:30pm or so. I get back inside and do some final detail on the bar before I flip the switch into gear to pour for any early arrivals.

The barback, Chris, comes up to me and let's me know that the band had asked him to ask me if they could use one of my 8" high ice tubs on the main stage, to ice up their chosen beverages during their performance. I always bring four or five of them with me, because you never know! I actually had one spare left that wasn't being used, so it was there's. They placed the tub in front on the DJ lift, where a drum kit would usually be, center-back.

I have to admit, I wasn't a big fan of the hip-hop music style, but I was definitely interested in hearing the groove of the set, with handy earplugs in my right pocket just to reduce the sound volume a smidgeon, being so close to the stage, almost part of it. The deep-heavy, low frequencies of the tall monitors, behind me and slightly to the left, were about to get tested, and so was I. His new album release of that year, The Blue Carpet Treatment, was probably going to be showcased in the set, along with many others. I would be at a loss to figure them out, anyway.

Where I was located, it happened to be in a good visual to see Kelly at her bar in the distance. It's too bad we didn't have ear pieces on the same channel so we could talk with each other. Guests slowly began to fill the main floor. My VIP section would start rolling heavy about 45 minutes later. By 10:00pm, it was like a big party. It was one of those paces behind the bar where I was in top form, my favorite speed, quick and agile, with fast hands, body warm, and a tanned smile.

When the decibel level of the music is high, like this event or any cracking nightclub, it is of benefit for me as a bartender to read lips when guests are telling me what they want to drink. Otherwise, my voice/vocal chords would be wasted by the end of the night. Sometimes, the best you can do is just to settle for a balanced usage of both. It all depends on how much people move their lips when they speak, some more or less than others. And above all, you're trying to help the guest in avoiding having to shout as well. If it can be reduced to any degree, it creates a calmer space.

It was show time. The lights dimmed. House music panned down. The intro music to the concert panned up from the soundboard. The Dogg Pound came on stage with the beginning delivery. Snoop entered from the same side of the stage where I was, and walked upstage to the center. The packed crowd was going crazy. There were no seats on the floor, all general admission. Spotlights beamed in various colors on the star of the show. The beat and the groove filled the house with everyone's bodies in the same motion. It became a big sweathouse of G-Funk music, drinks, and dancing.

I was soaked by the end of the night. The concert was about a 90-100 minute set. There may have been a midnight curfew or a little after, for this type of venue. It's still a little fuzzy to me all these years later at what time the show actually started, and what time the last encore was before the lights went up and liquor pouring stopped for the night.

It was good that Chris was backing me with consistent beverage fill-ups throughout the night. I got so freaking busy in VIP, it was like a race car barely keeping it in control on the track by just a hair, as the bartender for the in-crowd. I know there were many notables in the section, but you can't know everybody. Some of the ones I did recognize and that stepped up to the bar were NBA players Sam Cassell and Shaun Livingston from the L.A. Clippers. This was back just some months before Shaun had suffered that horrific knee injury in a game against the Charlotte Bobcats that almost ended his career. He was like the young kid hanging around and learning from Sam as a mentor. It was great to see, and Shaun was playing so good at that time.

Tara Reid came to the bar and hung out with me for a while during the night, as well as Jake Busey, Gary Busey's son. Jake was totally cool, even when I let him know that my favorite movie of his dad's was The Buddy Holly Story. All was good when Jake let me know that was his favorite too! Everyone was chillin'. Another part of my job, indirectly and especially working solo, is to set a good energy for the space with quality communication and good cheer, but to avoid giving too much attention to any one individual. Yet, having the few infrequent moments during the evening behind the bar when no one was asking for a drink was a brief relief where I could catch my breath and wits.

It was fitting for Snoop Dogg to do a show in a church setting, as he sang in a church choir when he was growing up. It was certainly a different atmosphere for me to be pouring drinks in as well. The night came to a closure, like they all do. I'm all too used to it, seeing the change that slowly happens from the beginning of the night to the somewhat intoxicated end. We all get to lose ourselves for awhile. It feels good, natural, a perfect environment for release of inhibition. There's something healthy about it. God knows we need it! But like anything we do, moderation is always a good key to hold onto, as excess in any direction tends to lead to an imbalance, which can also mean that if our workload gets to be too much at times in our lives, then all we really have to do is party till it starts moving back towards center, with whatever vices go along with it!

In my position behind the bar at a thousand parties and events, I serve and observe for the most part. Though, when or if the moment hits me during the course, I will loosen up even further and participate. It's all timing to me, as my energy is high-wired to perform with success, so I have to be careful of how much formula I add to the solution that's already been created to get to the finish line of any given night on a gig. Sometimes I do, other times I don't.

If there was a downside to this gig, it was the strange way in which the overall tip pool was handled at the end of the night. It had always been a good, fair experience working with Bar One, and I got along with the owners and staff very well. Let's put it this way. In an event of this size and nature, the owners relied on Jeffrey and myself to perform with our collective experience and knowledge, in the two high-profile bar positions of the night – the VIP sections.

It's why they chose us over others on staff, therefore fair and proper compensation needed to reflect that. My ring was high, and I raked in the tips big time, well over $1000, but I also did the work that deserved it, my barback as well. The end cut was shockingly low, as though they flattened it out and gave everyone the same pay. It was bullshit, and Jeffrey got hit the same way. I didn't mind sharing a substantial portion of it to help the cause, but other considerations should have been in play, and weren't. That was the beginning of the eventual end for me and Bar One. They fucked up, and didn't possess too much concern about it, except for the guilt in their eyes. That direct and close-up eye contact from me was a bitch for them. For the first time, they showed me a different face. It was a side of them I was hoping to never see.

I think all the staff probably felt a little chumped. Kelly and I grabbed our shit (bar kits) and walked out. I felt bad for her too. I brought her to it. We're walking on the sidewalk and I'm thinking to myself while steaming, "I hope my truck is still there when we slightly turn the corner and cross the street to the lot". This is downtown. It can be guarded, it cannot be guarded. I saw it from a distance and had a visual sigh. It's like my old horse. It's been through the mill like I have. 24 years on the road now. I'm not comfortable feeling like I've just left it tethered to a post for someone to trot off with it.

We arrive at the truck and I unlock the passenger door for Kelly. I'm glad I brought a change of shirt with me. It felt like a long drive home that night, doing so well at the bar, created a great vibe for the VIP pit, I dug them, they dug me, and then getting screwed really good at the end. Not quite the type of sex I was hoping for. Too bad there wasn't a second night of this same event, I would have considered fucking them back, from behind! See how they liked it.

This country still acts like the Wild West, which is why I have no problems with "An Eye for an Eye". Let's just say, I understand it. It's real old school! You know, like the shitheads in suits who've been systematically ruining this land for decades. Too bad I had no other choice but to take the high road, if you can even call it that. But the move they made with what they did is now in their biology whether they know it or not, and I'm okay with that too. Their demise is their choice, preferably sooner rather than later . . .

The City of Angels must've let a devil slip through to hover over the consecrated grounds of that historic and sacred building. Who knows, maybe a percentage of the total gratuity had to go as a tithing! Someone else's pocket other than the church, though.

3

MARTINIS AND MASSAGES

For the last few years, I've been working on the average of once a month at a retirement village in Thousand Oaks, at one time called Castle Hill, but has since been changed to The Reserve. The initial call came into Pierre of Pierre's Catering in Westlake, of whom I also work gigs with. He called me to ask if I wanted to do the gig, and that it may turn into something regular. They weren't requiring any food catering, as the property has its own kitchen and Chef on premise, so Pierre just handed it off to me. I checked the date in my calendar and I was open, so I went ahead and gave them a call. The gig was set.

In talking on the phone with Jolene, the Activities Director, she told me the various management on staff were starting a get-together on the last Thursday of each month, a mixer-of-sorts to network with directors of other facilities in and around the area that have to do with taking care of the elderly, in hopes of talking over unresolved issues they each may be having within their own positions, as well as thinking together of ways to improve areas of their work responsibility that are in need. The exchange of ideas while relaxing with a drink and a massage. Good idea!

The little event was called "Martinis & Massages". It was only for a few hours tops, and I have no problem with that. They pay, I pour! They also hired a licensed masseuse to come in and give everyone who came to the meeting of the minds a complimentary 20-minute massage, located in a small room right on the corner of the open space and hallway where it was all taking place. My bar set-up was a roomy built-in kitchen with a big countertop and hanging glassware. It was everything I needed.

Each month I would be creating a few different martinis, and some other cocktails once in a while, depending on the season. They had an ice machine, and I emailed them my full dry and wet stock beverage list on a word doc. We were ready to go. My bar kit was laid out on the countertop in a nice, attractive design with the mats, the four shakers, and the whole shebang.

There were only 25 or so people invited each month, and we'd usually get about 15 showing up. The Chef would set up a small buffet, and there was even a popcorn machine in the hallway. It was a 5-7 pm event, but I would get there earlier to set-up, and would usually leave at about 7:30 or a little after, following clean-up.

Some of the retired citizens living on the property would come by and I made them drinks too. It is a beautiful thing to see them still enjoying a good cocktail whenever they have the chance, just something to help elevate their day, and they don't have to drive. It's like living in a resort for them. No worries! It's a nice reminder of when they used to frequent the happening bars, restaurants and nightclubs in their heyday of the 40's, 50's, etc.

I still see this 100-year old Texas woman that comes up to me and says hi, and orders a straight gin martini with olives, or on occasion a fruit-flavored martini when she wants to try something new. She walks around with no assistance of any kind for the most part, but at times you may see her with a cane if she feels a little weak or out of balance on any given day. But the woman's got a backbone like no tomorrow! She reminds me of my mother a little bit in that department. Most of the residents are in their 70's and older, and there's just under 200 that live in the community. They come from many walks of life, and have all kinds of interesting stories to tell. If I only had the time!

The Martinis & Massages event lasted for a good year or more before some things started to change with the corporation that owned it, and unfortunately some of the staff. It was a good run with that, but they also have me bartend all their other resident events that happen throughout the year, which is why I'm still needed there. It's also handy that I have my own custom portable bar when these parties are held outside on the two terraces, front and back.

One interesting thing occurred in early 2009. The Sales Director of then Castle Hill saw the new 2009 cocktail calendars that I produced, as I gave them each one as a gift for the new year. I had one of them set-up on the bar for display, and the director started asking me about creating a company brand calendar for Castle Hill and the other three properties that were owned. I was completely able to produce brand merch in this calendar product form and was looking forward to gaining orders in that area aside from my annual calendar releases.

She put in an order for 250 of them, and requested it be a special 18-month edition, starting in July of 2009 and going to the end of 2010. Done! The extra cards fit in the fold-out CD jewel box perfectly, and they came out great. Ron and I did a good job with the production and packaging. Since then, we've produced a calendar for a staffing company and created a Patron cocktail calendar for the brand's future consideration. To see the line of cocktail calendars, simply go to my website.

Though it's a very different environment to consider pouring drinks behind a bar in, it's also the greatest pleasure to chat with the elderly. They are so wise, kind, and patient. There are also ones that have a humorous mischief about them, including an old Italian man that moves around with his walker, whether near the bar/kitchen where I'm at, or in the main dining room for the residents, and snags any can sodas he can find by putting them in his walkers' canvas pouch when he's leaving. It's hilarious to see, especially when watching his eyes. He's on a carbonated beverage mission! His favorites are root beer and ginger ale. Then there's the talkative lady who is a retired dancer and actress, and the man who brings a Ziploc bag of jalapeno-filled olives for the straight gin martinis that I make him.

I still think today that this type of location and life that goes on here day-to-day would be a great comedy/drama series for primetime television. I saw a movie last year through Netflix called "Stanley's Gig", that took place here in Los Angeles, where the male lead played by the great character actor, William Sanderson (Bob Newhart Show, Blade Runner, Lonesome Dove, Deadwood, many others), was a musician hired into an assisted living complex a few times a week to entertain the residents, with one particular lady being a famous jazz singer from the 50's/60's era of the Central Avenue sounds.

Some time ago I had tried to get in on an on-call basis with an assisted living facility located an efficient five minutes from where I live, but they didn't have a need for my private/freelance services. It's the old Motion Picture & Television Country House and Hospital over on Mulholland Drive just across the South side of the 101 freeway in Calabasas, on the cusp of Woodland Hills. This 40-acre spread that was once walnut and orange groves, as was this whole area where I also live, which includes two walnut trees in the back yard, was opened in 1942 as a retirement community, with individual cottages, and a fully licensed acute-care hospital. Mary Pickford and Jean Hersholt broke the first ground.

The Motion Picture Hospital was dedicated on the grounds in 1948. Some of the many stars who attended were Ronald Reagan,

Shirley Temple, and Robert Young. The fees for living in the community were based solely on the "ability to pay". The minimum age is 70 for application in. All working in the business are accepted, from actors, artists, backlot men, cameramen, directors, producers, stars, to extras and security guards.

If only the Food & Beverage/Hospitality business, an equally important industry, would learn to take care of their own in the same way!

Scores of movie notables spent their last years there, including Bud Abbott, Mary Astor, Ellen Corby (Grandmother on The Waltons), Robert Cummings, Norman Fell (The Graduate, Bullitt, Catch-22, and as landlord Mr. Roper on Three's Company), Curly Howard (Three Stooges), Johnny Weissmuller (who also designed the big lap pool at Lakeside Golf Club, where I worked from 99'-02'), Hattie McDaniel (Mammie in Gone With The Wind), Joel McCrea, DeForest Kelley (Dr. McCoy on Star Trek), Edgar Kennedy (master of the slow burn), and the gorgeous Yvonne DeCarlo (Lily Munster on *The Munsters* TV series).

Did I tell you that I love old Hollywood? Yes, I think I've mentioned it in a few other stories. The history is just more interesting and rich to me.

I still get called in to work bar-needed functions at what's now known as The Reserve, for many of their monthly resident events and holiday gatherings either inside the main room or outside on the back terrace. They'll have singers, jazz bands, or even a recent Beatles tribute band hired to perform. They have a budget for occasional parties, so they have the money to work with.

Everyone has gotten to know me over the last several years, so it's a mutual appreciation, and they like having me there so I can make some of the classic cocktails and many other drinks, or just having a bartender behind a bar available for them once in a while is a good feeling, for them and myself.

4

SWINGTOWN

It was an early Friday afternoon in the Fall of 2007, my favorite weather outside, in the 70's. At this point I had pretty much given up hope of getting booked on a gig for that evening, as nothing came in during the week to fill the vacant spot. It happens once in a while on a weekend night when you work the way I do. Many times with on-call gigs, even though I end up getting enough overall, can still run feast or famine. I did a couple gigs during the week, and had one scheduled for Saturday as well.

Unexpectedly, I get a call from Gary at a place I freelanced called Club Red, just down the boulevard about three miles from where I live, a nice club space that held about 200 people, including the back outside patio. I had worked there during a previous owner, and that's how I got back into their bartender rotation. There's always someone who needs a night off, is out of town, leaves, or is sick. That's where I come in.

Gary asked if I could work for a closed doors private party from a group who had rented the club out for the night. Perfect! I fill the week up and all I have to do is drive down the street and arrive about 8:00pm. I said yes, but didn't ask anything more over the phone. Gary and his brother and father operated the club. They were of Eastern European descent, and I got along with them fine. I can basically work with anyone, as long as they allow me to do my job.

Many owners and managers can be a little sketchy of some of their staff, unsure of trust. With my resume, the reputation I had helped them be more comfortable with me. After I had wrote an article about the bar, titled "Sexy in Red", which made it into the previous year's June issue of Patterson's Beverage Journal, that further solidified their faith in me. This club is also the place where they allowed me to have a photo shoot done behind the bar for a feature cover story titled "Luminous Layers" with Sante Magazine, that came out in the September 08' issue.

So this is cool, I had about six hours till showtime. I was motivated! Get a couple loads of laundry done, clean up the place a bit, and as the sun came through the trees in the backyard around 4:00pm, I set-up the cycling wind trainer on the sundeck, and with my racing bike locked in and headphones on jamming to some heavy rock, I saddled up and unloaded an endurance workout for about 45 minutes non-stop.

I have a huge music library with almost a thousand recorded mixes that I've taped as a hobby for close to 30 years, so I throw one of those in, and as soon as the cassette is done, so am I. Figure it equates to about an 8-mile haul for the exercise, but without the cars and inclines. I shower, then order a pizza and relax for a while watching a couple disc episodes from a TV show through Netflix.

Dusk to dark, it's time for me to suit up and roll. I love it when my gig is five minutes away from home. When you've traversed the roads and canyons of the valley and over the hill of L.A. like I have for so long, it's so nice not to be putting a round-trip of 30-40 miles on the speedometer all the time, especially in shit traffic.

I arrive and park where I always do, in back of the boulevard and club, in an unknown-to-the-eye parking-paved alley, that is basically a fence between and 20 feet away from the 101 freeway. I always get there 10 minutes early so I can gather my bar kit, put my shirt on, and have a smoke leaning against the truck while I observe the back of the club from a distance, feeling the energy to psyche up for the night.

Getting inside, I greet everyone, and start setting up my liquor well in the main bar, not really paying much attention to anyone except for what the barback is getting done. The coolers and kegs look ready to go, and ice is on the way. I finish positioning other bottles and juices near the well to my preference. If I haven't been there for awhile, other bartenders put their liquid gear in various areas of placement depending on how ambidextrous they work , if they're southpaws, or still building their hand-eye coordination. Only one out of one hundred people are naturally ambidextrous, so it can take some longer than others to get their moves down in a fast, fluid motion, along with figuring out where everything in and around the well should go for quick memory access while pouring on-the-fly.

I'm lucky in that I was easily adaptable to this type of work, being built-for-speed and thinking on my feet. In batting cages, I would always end up batting both right and left before I finished. And with being good in many sports, my physical aptitude and level of awareness was a good fit for this occupation. But for my brain to function correctly, I have to practice a sense of order to a large degree, in both my personal and professional life. I'm an efficiency freak, so I need mental clearance to engage my gears for optimal performance, or I might as well not even attempt it. Especially nowadays, after three decades behind the bar, it can sometimes take that much to focus for lock and load, because my wheels are spinning too fast, too often, and paying the price for it. But once I shift to engage . . . . I'm in for the long haul.

I'm there for about 20 minutes or so, and Gary comes up to me at the bar. I've worked hundreds of parties here, there and everywhere, so it really doesn't matter what the event is for the most part. I still get ready to rock the same way. It's the one good thing about setting up beforehand, it gets me in the mood to groove. Then, Gary gives me the unexpected lowdown. The group of people who rented the entire space all belong to a swinger's club that are coming together from a few surrounding states as a chosen annual destination. I go "Oh . . . okay!" Gary grins, and I start chuckling a bit. I now understood why the house lights were dimmed down further than usual!

Yanni was bartending with me, in another well, and a newbie was working the small bar on the other side of the club, as Tonya and Julia weren't interested in gigging this theme night behind the bar. It was no problem for us slinging voyeurs! We were just bummed that the deep corners and booths were pitch dark. This also made the under-bar running lights look brighter than normal, so our faces would reflect an increase in glowing, much like the bartender in the ballroom of the movie "The Shining", when our legs were up against the wells speed rack, making drinks.

Married couples and single couples were arriving through the two rear entrances, as well as the front door, open for a short period of time at the start. The DJ created an atmosphere with a specially-designed style and set of music for the night, and the two wall screens activated with shadow dancers. Soon enough, we were on the journey.

As we were getting busy at the bar, things started to slowly heat up and get . . . umm . . . visually interesting, curious as to what the dress code would not be! If there was ever a time to have night vision glasses on, you know, just for observation purposes and to be educated on this group's standards and practices, now was the time.

Matching, mingling, and mixing it up like strangers in the night, dressed in black or some deep, sharp colors, in leather, in lace and beads, heels and boots, and sexy lingerie, with the simple tone of less is more. I'm finding myself watching the movement of the candlelight in the distant periphery, and a candelabra standing tall and alone in the dark toward the back center of the stage, all the while making drinks and serving them up close and personal.

There are well over 100 swingers clubs in the Los Angeles and surrounding areas alone, with names like The Hush Hush Club, The Cougar's Den, Passion Palace, Tangerine's Dream, and Country Erotica to mention a few. Quite the underground lifestyle, though with the internet, is anything really underground anymore?

It was only a matter of time and a few drinks before the ladies started to flirt with us pretty heavy at the bar. They weren't holding back much when it came to telling us of their interests. Yanni and I always looked good and worked well behind the bar together, but that also lends itself to looking single in our positions as well, which seemed to possess a bit of a turn on for some of the women. Inquiring further with us, it was revealed that a couple of them were interested in a threesome of sorts. I'm sure a tasting of that nature was not out of their options to consider, trade or no trade. Eventually their boyfriends or husbands would come to the rescue and get them back on point.

I remember Yanni and I taking turns now and then walking out of the bar and into the depths of the floor, making an excuse to go over to the other bar, gazing about to see the action going on in other corners. We also had a cocktail waitress on the floor. I hadn't seen her in a while, and she was always a breath of beauty to behold. A Rosario Dawson-type, Latin and hotter than hell. Half the time I couldn't keep my eyes off her whenever she came up and ordered drinks. She was super-nice, and we got along great. She always wanted me to teach her how to tend bar. I can only imagine what abrupt close-ups and encounters she ran into during the night. But she was down for it !

There was definitely some serious heavy petting, kissing, caressing, stroking, licking and talking dirty close to the ear on the agenda. But the dim-lit environment created a sense of being discreet and not out in a lighted open area, like some sexual orgy for everyone to see, reflecting a feel that sets them apart from wilder forms of sexual activity and get-togethers, still holding on to some level of romantic nuance in their overall intentions.

Maybe there are no rules, certainly not with the degree of foreplay we noticed with the guest activity at the club, just when they get back to their hotel suites at 3:00am. Then the game changes slightly to something more . . . protected and safe.

It was an interesting evening of entertainment and communication. It's like we got to watch a free show, and get paid for it! For this night, the one thing you may not want to see is for the house lights to go up too far when it's closing time. It would be better to have most of the guests on their way out while the lights are still low, avoiding any unnecessary exposures of any kind before they get whatever clothing back on that they took off.

Another bar gig in the books for me. The more variety of theme and event, the better. However, this was a night to . . . well . . . never forget!

The club has been closed for the last couple years now. The Ukrainians soon disappeared, thankfully not owing me anything. Something was supposed to open up there at the beginning of this year, but it never happened. So the space sits empty today.

It also goes to note that just a few months after that club night, Julia ended up getting a day job at the Donald Sterling Corporation (L.A. Clippers, etc.), and Tonya is now the personal assistant to the actor, Hugh Laurie (House, etc.).

It's the way of the Food and Beverage business in the City of Angels. Establishments rise and fall constantly. Things move on and we all go our different ways . . . . . sometimes meeting up again elsewhere unexpectedly.

5

RIDE A ROCK HORSE

In mid-September of 2009, I get a call from Emily at Patron Tequila to book me as the main bartender at a sponsored event for the first week in October, happening in the backyard of a private residence in Pacific Palisades, an auction-fundraiser for the Autism Foundation. The date was open in my calendar, so I penciled it in.

It was a very high-end party, a $2500-a-plate type of evening, whether it was per/person or per/couple, I never found out. The night's musical entertainment was none other than The Who's legendary singer, Roger Daltrey, and his band which included Pete Townsend's brother, Simon, on guitar. The special guests were going to be Dave Stewart (Eurythmics) and Joss Stone. Quite the highlight to be a part of! With a show of this magnitude, a slew of well-to-do's and celebs were sure to be in attendance.

The next few weeks of bar gigs went by at a brisk pace, and soon enough it was time to rock the Ice Bar for Patron once again. I knew Roland and Dan from Carving Ice would be there setting up their custom artistic delivery of frozen water design for me to work with, so we'd get a chance to chat and catch up, as it's only a few times a year where were on the same gigs together.

On the way there from the far west side of the valley, I ditch the house early with dress clothes and all necessary bar gear in tow, trek through Topanga Canyon to PCH, hang a left down the stunning coast highway for a few miles, and trip up the California Incline into Santa Monica. The primary mission anytime I get back over to work in this part of town is to roll up Wilshire Boulevard and 26 Street to my favorite Mexican muncheria, Casa Escobar, for an enchilada dinner before the night work begins on my own stage, the show before the show!

It's never a good idea to walk into a gig hungry, hoping you can rely on the caterer to slide you appetizers throughout the evening. If it's one thing the outfits that hire me know, is that I don't care to fill my mouth with food while I'm behind the bar serving guests. Not a good sight to be presenting. Though they wouldn't mind if I did a little, they also appreciate that I don't partake, especially when John Paul is around.

After the heavenly bite to eat and an ice tea as a roadie, I was building up that feeling of full power. It felt good, yet kind of anxious to get the party started, I knew the early prep work at the bar would keep my feet firmly planted on the ground with position in perspective. I arrive and park on the street around 4:15 pm, and lit up a smoke while walking around to the passenger door to look over the gear to make sure I didn't forget anything. In L.A., if you space to take something with you, never-mind, because you won't be going back to get it. The city's just too big, and traffic is neither loving nor forgiving.

At a distance, I hear the humming sound of the power generators coming from the 18-wheeler parked up on the corner of the cross street, toward what would be the back of the house. Walking up the steps of this amazingly-designed modern home with parts of my full bar kit over both shoulders, I make a right and head to the backyard. Other set-up people are moving in every direction.

Like a horse gnawing on grass, I keep the visual of my spearmint gum chewing to a minimum, but it helps to get my motor running in tune, and keeps my breath fresh. It's still bright as hell outside, so I have my sunglasses on like many around do, dealing with our sensitive-to-light issues from living the vampire life of night workers on the L.A. party circuit, and in clubs till crazy hours under the moon.

We work everywhere. Many of us who have years and years of experience in this line of employment are hampered with old, sometimes re-occurring injuries that we would never show, and only speak to each other about. We hide it well. Many of them are here, so I don't feel alone in my occasional, silent pains. And the majority of us do not have any health insurance, not when you work the way we do. It's unfortunate that there isn't something in place to take care of this necessity when using both physical and mental capacities. But when it costs the same as a monthly payment on a brand new car when procuring it on your own, it's just plain unaffordable to comfortably fit into a budget with a terrible economy.

Holy Shit! A full stage set-up, just like a band on tour, and wired for sound. I hoped the event hosts gave plenty of advance notice to all the neighbors in the close and surrounding residential, regardless of property size. The potential decibel level of the music was bound to range above the trees and out a ways.

The guest count was going to be close to 200, so with that alone times the ticket price, plus the incredible auction items, would gather up to be a large sum for total monies raised. It couldn't fail!

I met up with Emily, and she gave me the lowdown on the ground play. Someone's in the Kitchen was the chosen food caterer, out of Tarzana, of whom I've actually worked with before in the past, so it was cool to see a few familiar faces still with them. One of their bartenders, Rob, was going to be working alongside me, stationed at the custom double-luge ice bar located about 25 feet to the left of the stage, making martinis all night long for the guests. There was another Patron long regular bar area across the way from us that was going to be worked by a few other bartenders from the caterer.

Martinis meant real martini glasses, so there was no plastic for simpler stacking and usage. Our backbar space was going to be tight with product, tubs, ice, and an endless rotation of semi-stackable and always-fragile glassware. It was tough for me and Rob to initially get the *mise en place* underway for that area, as the guys from Carving Ice were also right there in arms touch, slowly building the blocks of the ice bar together. We had to stay out of their way while trying to do our job as well. With a melting bar like this, we also stand and walk on a custom-built bar riser, between the bar and backbar, so the luge-pouring is at a more accessible height. Below the bar is a huge catch-drain.

After being on site for about 40 minutes, roaming around getting a lay of the land and where everything was, Daltrey shows up with a couple of friends, walking casually in through the yard and eventually toward the stage. Many of us took an extra breath like some form of time stand still. The band members were already on stage tuning and adjusting. Roger hopped up and within minutes they engage in a sound check with a run-through of a few songs, which included "Who Are You", and all for us hard-working staffers.

How cool is that, a legend in the midst hanging out with us on a beautiful late afternoon, and jamming. Like we hear and say to ourselves many times living in the city of angels – "Only in LA!"

What nobody there knew, is when I worked as a music rack jobber for a distributor called All Label West in Phoenix during the early 80's before my move to Los Angeles, the CEO of the company at that time was The Who's tour manager in the late 60's, named Bill. Talk about a small world!

Rob and I were close to getting the bar prep detail finished about the same time as the ice bar came to completion. And what a beauty it was to behold, another masterful job by Dan and Roland. And to think that they travel on the freeway from Anaheim to this hour-away destination point with it still frost-frozen in the truck, the ultimate engineers of ice sculpture and temperature stability in the warm west.

With some time to spare before we opened the bar for service, I took a walk back out to the truck to wipe the sweat off, change into my work shirt after a quick swipe of the speed stick, and had another smoke. It was nice out, the weather was going to be perfect for this evening. It's a performance for us as well, as when you work out in the fields like this, you never know who you're going to be serving. Every face is new and fresh, people you've never met or seen before.

Rob and I had prepped and pitcherized a few of the recipes to make it easy on ourselves when it came to shaking and pouring down the luge. All we had were martini glasses, and a few shot and rocks glasses to work with, so things were streamlined pretty well for us. The sun went down past the high trees on the other side of the house, so we avoided, along with the bar, burning in the shine.

Guests started rolling in and soon we were off and running, drinks going out as fast as we could make them. There's a big difference in an early rush when it comes to people arriving in a staggered process by way of their own vehicle vs. getting dropped off by a shuttle or a bus. Luckily, there was a valet just outside on the street, so we didn't have to deal with blocks of 50 guests hitting us at once.

It wasn't long before the party was in full swing. A variety of appetizers were being tray-passed all around, the house music was up, and everyone enjoying themselves with a cocktail in their hands. The emcee of the night took the stage around the 75-90 minute mark of the cocktail hour, greeted everyone, and gave them the warm rundown of the evening's festivities, along with highlighting some of the special items up for auction, and introduced the representative of the Autism Foundation, who had some kind and hopeful words to say, along with some updates and thanks.

There was a non-material item up for grabs, and maybe the most challenging of the night, if not memorable for a lifetime. Guests would get to wager on getting up on stage and singing background vocals with Daltrey, when him and his band would perform the song "My Generation", with their continuous line to sing over and over again being "Talkin' bout my generation". Very cool! Hard to screw up those lyrics, even after a few drinks, it would help.

After more guest mingling and serving, it must've been 10:00pm or so when Roger finally hit the stage for the band to perform their set, though it wouldn't have mattered how long. Any length of time would be worth the wait for this.

The show was great, and sounded really good as well. I wrote every song down in sequence on a cocktail napkin. Below is the song setlist of the show:

Who Are You

I Can See For Miles

Pictures of Lily

Behind Blue Eyes

The Healer

I Wanna Be Your Rider

2000 Years

Days of Light (from his 92' solo album "Rocks in the Head")

Ring of Fire (Johnny Cash cover)

My Generation

Pinball Wizard

Baba O'Reilly

Dave Stewart and Joss Stone came on stage in the middle of the set and did a couple acoustic-electric blues numbers, the last one being a cover of "You Really Got a Hold on Me". The daughters of the host of the party won the opportunity to sing "My Generation". It was perfect in a way, having the young girls with a little rowdy in them getting up there to share a microphone. It turned out awesome, and all of us were singing along anyway, so even this couldn't turn bad!

The show that Roger did in San Francisco just a week after our event, gives a good feel and sense of what it was like when he performed for us, of which you can check out on YouTube.

Rob took the bar over for me when I departed for a while to get closer to the stage for the encore songs, but I really just stayed out on the perimeter, as it was pretty packed there right up in front. Standing over to the right of me in front about five feet were Jim Carrey and Jenny McCarthy. He had long hair and a grown-out beard. Both were dressed down and dark a bit, a less recognizable style, but it was cool. When the last song ended, we turned around, and as I was walking back to the bar, I heard Jim say "Crazy!". He was right, though. It was such a surreal moment to see a show of this caliber in a backyard, however large and equipped it may have been.

The end of the show was the beginning of the slow fade-out of the party. This was a weekday night, not a weekend, so people felt the need to get back home for some hours of sleep for the morning rise to work. However, with well over a half-million dollars raised in one night to assist families with their autistic children, it couldn't have been a more happier ending.

Rob and I break down and pack up the backbar, including the leftover bottles of the precious Vitamin T, while Roland and Dan's work assistants start deconstructing what's left of the full ice bar, making sure nothing falls of its own liquid weakening. It can happen, but it's usually the top parts that go first for reasons of usage, as the bottom parts of the bar are the thickest blocks.

We helped Emily load up her truck with some Patron product and merch, more the remains of the other bars than ours. She was topped off, so I ended up loading whatever was left in my truck, getting it back to the main office whenever I got called on the next gig, or sometimes just bringing it to the next event for use, depending on the where and when.

What a great event this was . . . . . makes the night ride home back down and along PCH to Topanga . . . an ocean breeze.

6

Finyl Vinyl

It was one of those hot and humid August evenings, back in 2008. I was driving into Hollywood and getting off on the Vine Street exit. Traffic was so-so. I made a quick left on the first street I came to in order to get over to Argyle, making a right and then another quick right was the way into the back entrance and gated parking lot of the famous Capitol Records Tower.

Built in 1956 to match its state-of-the-art Abbey Road Studios in London shortly after EMI acquired majority stock of Capitol, the world's first circular office building, resembling a stack of 45's on a turntable, was also earthquake-resistant for it's time. The old Landmark Hotel in Las Vegas, before it was torn down, was also a similar style. The blinking light atop the tower spells out the name "Hollywood" in Morse code every few seconds, and has ever since the tower was open.

The timing was good. I had to be there at 6:00 pm. Earlier in the week, I had received a call from one of the marketing research firms that I'm connected with here in town, as I like to participate in focus groups. You get paid really well for these, and they're only for a couple hours. The group I made it into for the same day as

40

the Capitol gig was in Valley Village and ended about 5:15 pm, giving perfect time for me to scoot into Tinseltown afterwards.

This session had to do with giving our opinions on a new television show that hadn't aired yet. There were about 50 of us. We go into this small custom-built theatre and watch the episode that they select for us to see. Each of us hold a -/+ control box at our seats that tells them if we like or dislike the show, or some particular part of it, as they monitor it all the way through. We fill out a few pages of more specifics when the episode is finished, get paid, and we're gone.

Right underneath the wheels of my truck in the parking lot are the famous Capitol echo chambers; eight subterranean concrete bunkers located 30 feet underground. Custom-built in the 60's, the engineers on the ground floor studios can simply pipe in whatever degree of real physical reverberation they want or need for the music, permitting an echo effect lasting up to five seconds.

On one end of the chamber are the speakers, the other end the microphones. Something tells me there's a below-ground studio floor as well! At the time, Capitol's producers felt the Beatles recordings were sonically unsuited to the U.S. market, so they significantly altered the content by adding equalization to brighten the sound, but also piped the recordings through the echo chamber.

It was my first time in. I was jazzed about stepping into music recording history. The gig came through Tender Bartenders via Wendy Koro, a food catering client of Tabi's, so I knew a couple of the food staffers who were going to be there, including Kathy Orrico, one of my favorite peeps to work with. Koro and Orrico ? Of course, that can't not happen ! Together, they're Wendy Kathy Korrico !!

At the artist entrance, there was a small lobby desk to check in with right after you walk in the door, to get my badge for the evening. Everything as it should be, and expected. This was one of those short and small get-togethers of 30-40 people with no major announcements, an artist EP CD wrap party with musicians, managers, family and a few friends, as they were finishing up with completing tracks and/or final mixing in the studio for the evening.

Walking through the old narrow hallways of this musical shrine, I'm thinking if these walls could only talk. Could this landmark be haunted? Carrying my bar pack over my shoulder, I'm making sure to avoid knocking it against anything hanging on the grey walls, high or low.

I follow one of the cater girls up a set of tight steps to one of the lounge rooms where there's an island bar top I would use as my prep-and-pour station, along with a back wall kitchen counter and sink for the food execution. It's an okay space, but I have to keep in mind that every area of the building's interior is extremely old school. There's no doubt that musicians back in the day with any height or width to them left the tower with some head or shoulder bruising. No wonder musicians wore hats more back in the day! This was back when stairs of any kind were built almost ladder-like, as opposed to the safer, more gradual degrees of incline today. It would be almost crawl space for someone like the late, great saxophonist, Clarence Clemons, until they made it into the actual studio.

After prepping the bar, I sneak out for a few minutes and go back downstairs. I make a left and walk right into Studio A. There were a few musicians hanging out on the other side, but I just stood there and took it all in for a minute. The history of all the major talent that's recorded in these studios is mind-boggling. It was nicknamed "The House That Nat Built" to recognize the enormous contributions of Nat "King" Cole. The studios were designed by guitarist and legendary sound expert, Les Paul.

The hallways are laced with black & white pictures in 8 ½ x 11 frames and gold records with the likes of Nat "King" Cole, Frank Sinatra, Judy Garland, Nancy Wilson, Dean Martin, The Beach Boys, Glen Campbell, The Band, Grand Funk Railroad, Bob Seger, Tina Turner, Steve Miller Band, Bonnie Raitt, Green Day, Everclear, Megadeth, and so many more. Capitol also developed a jazz line that issued the Miles Davis-led sessions called "Birth of the Cool". John Lennon's star on the Hollywood Walk of Fame is just outside the building, and Country superstar Garth Brooks has his star outside the front door.

It was Johnny Mercer, the great songwriter (Skylark, Moon River, One For My Baby, I'm Old Fashioned, Come Rain or Come Shine, I Remember You, Charade, That Old Black Magic, many more) along with film producer Buddy DeSylva who founded and created Capitol Records back in 1942. Mercer also brought in his friend, Glenn Wallichs, for his business knowledge from owning the biggest record store in Los Angeles, Music City, located on the corner of Sunset and Vine, which was open from 1940-1978.

So, if you noticed the dates, Capitol was in the recording business for 13 years at another location prior to the tower being constructed.

Wendy and the girls were working behind and all around me. Though I love that, I really don't care to have the food so close when I'm making drinks. There were no windows or outdoor fresh air. With one small ventilation fan, the variety of hot appetizers prepped in the mini-oven and so on, there's a foodie combination stench in the air that is displeasing with my nose to say the least, almost made me want to throw up in my mouth.

The food was fine, it's the aromas that just need a place to dissipate quicker out of the occupied air space. I took a drink of club soda, hoping that would help a little. I don't know what the specific smell is, something with too much butter accent, but it gets me every time where I have to walk out of the room for a minute. The girls just glide through it like their nostrils are on shutdown mode. Too many staffers for this gig made for an over-packed corral with bumper car-like floor choreography.

It was cool to just hang out and make good drinks for everyone. There was no big plan, just simple and sweet. I didn't know who the artist was, and neither did anyone else working the gig. I'm sure Capitol has seen plenty a share of talented unknowns come through the doors to record over the decades in hopes of making it big. A place, among others, where artists get signed and give it their best shot.

The studios still operate today at its West Coast office, even though in 2006 EMI sold the tower and adjacent properties for $50 million to New York-based developer Argent Ventures. As of May of this year, The Millennium Hollywood project is now back on the table, who along with Argent, plan on building a mixed-use complex that would take three years to complete if the city approves it, that would include two skyscrapers around the tower, all in an attempt to restore Hollywood's glamour and charm it had in the 1930's and 40's.

Don't know if skyscrapers would do that sort of thing! Guess it all depends on the look and feel. However, the tower and studio would not be endangered, as the building is now an historical monument, and the new owners want to preserve it as such. We'll see what happens . . .

Today, the rumor in town is that the top half of the Capitol building is slated to be turned into lofts. I'm guessing that'll equate to 6-8 living spaces, one loft per/floor. I just can't see the floors being shared/split in half to make two per/floor, as the building itself is not that big. It's also close to the Hollywood freeway, which may or may not be a detracting point, but I know from up there in the higher floors, you'll get a surrounding view of the city.

I'm glad I made it in one time before everything changes for good. Visiting Capitol was right up my alley. In my late teens and early 20's, I had worked in record stores, as a rack jobber with two music distribution companies, and completed a 6-week basics course at a recording engineering school. The only thing I wish I would have done is ask one of the security guards if they could take me up to one of the top floors, just so I could take a quick look around.

Outside in the parking lot with the tail gate down on my truck, I sat and chatted with Kathy for about 15 minutes, sharing a smoke and talking about our week's other gig work coming up. It also gave us a few minutes to just get a good, close-up look at the cylindrical building at night. Capitol has never conducted tours in the tower, so we felt pretty lucky getting an inside glimpse, if only for a few hours.

7

THE PAJAMA GAME

There are some gigs I work that are total mysteries. When I book a party with a client, private or otherwise, I get the basic details, but I make a point not to ask for too much information over the phone or by email in advance. However, the larger the event is usually equates to extra Intel. But this was not one of them. The theme of this get-together that took place on a late summer night in 2008 was a little different than the many I've worked in the past.

In the far outskirts of the valley and on the Ventura County line, only 3 minutes and 1½ miles away from where I live, there's the super rich and relaxed gated community and incorporated city of Hidden Hills, a population of about 2,000. Its design and development off the 101 freeway in the 1950s gives the feel even more today of "so close, yet so far away".

The rustic, pastoral atmosphere is witnessed by the absence of sidewalks and street lights, and replaced with white three-rail fences and bridle trails, convenient for the equestrian lifestyle, as the land sitting next to Hidden Hills to the north is the 3,000 acre Upper Las Virgenes Canyon Open Space Preserve (the former working Ahmanson Ranch, of which I just recently bartended a wedding up there a few weeks ago), with miles of trails that horse-owning residents in the community simply enter through a secret gate of their own to get into.

A country way of life in the city! Who could ask for anything more?

Back in the 20s and 30s the then 4,000 acres was known as Lasky Mesa. Many historic movies were filmed in this undeveloped location of rolling hills and wide-open spaces, including *Gone With the Wind, The Thundering Herd, The Charge of the Light Brigade, They Died With Their Boots On. Silver Spurs, Santa Fe Trail, Duel in the Sun, and Wild Heritage.*

Today, Hidden Hills is one of the top wealthiest communities in America, with the strongest concentration of upper-end incomes. When you've seen many of these amazing properties of which I've been fortunate, one quickly understands that you have to be well-off to get in here, but even more important to have a passion for the surroundings.

What I like the most is the cool and laid-back feel the residents have. It reminds me of when I grew up on a farm in the country at an early age back in upstate New York, so I kind of feel at home, and am about as close as I'll ever get to it unless I win the lotto. For now, I have no problem with them paying the bills.

I've worked the bar at many private parties/events within the gates, a very convenient location for me. They know me, I know them. We know each other! By just cruising around the streets inside the main drag of Long Valley Road, you would never guess there are close to 600 homes within this little city. It was also the setting of the short-lived NBC sitcom *Hidden Hills* which aired in 2002-2003. Maybe it would have lasted longer if it was a drama? Going way back, Wes Craven's 1978 horror film *Summer of Fear* aka "Stranger in Our House", was filmed in the community.

Many celebs have lived here at one time or another or now, including Neil Diamond, Powers Boothe (Deadwood, 24, Tombstone, Emerald Forest), Alex Van Halen, Melissa Etheridge, Ernie Hudson (OZ, Ghostbusters), Josh Satin of the New York Mets lives here and was born here, Will Smith and Jada Pinkett, Cuban trumpet player Arturo Sandoval, Denise Richards, Billy Blanks (Tae Bo), Matt Leblanc, Ozzy and Sharon Osbourne, Jennifer Lopez, Lisa Marie Presley, Shaun Cassidy, Mark Isham (legendary film composer), Howie Mandel, Bruce Jenner, the Kardashians, and now Britney Spears in her massive 20,000 sq.ft. mansion.

I'm winding through some off-shoot streets and arrive at the address to the party in good time. With roads named Kit Carson, John Muir, Jed Smith, and Annie Oakley, it quickly makes you feel down home. My first time here, I walk up the steep driveway and notice the home was one of maybe only a couple log homes built in the entire community. I love log homes and cabins. Very cool! Always nice to get a client referral . . .

Though they have a small custom-built bar in the main living room, the client, Debbie, took me outside to the backyard as I would be setting up my bar camp on the perfect and larger space of the barbeque island. The curves of the countertop design made it easily double as a big bar top. From scratch once again, here I go.

Grabbing several products from the inside bar and frig, along with some fine bottles of wine, fruit and essentials from the cooler in the garage along with the ice bags, and then, the glassware. Prepping outside, I noticed some vineyard growth off in the distant hill coverage, but hesitated on inquiring early on. Some things you just wait and see. There was no hurry in knowing, figuring at some point it would come around in conversation.

In meeting Debbie's husband, who was cool and hip, I soon realized by accidental overhear that he was going to be taking off and gone for most of the night. Some minutes later I asked Debbie what the occasion was, and she said I would probably enjoy it, as it was a get-together of 35-40 lady friends for a pajama party.

Nodding, I couldn't help but getting a slight grin on my face, what it looked like I had no idea, but as I tried to walk away and back to the duty-at-hand while hiding my facial expression, she started laughing and said "You're going to be the only man here tonight!"

God help me!   Sundown, you'd better take care . . .

With great weather to be had, there was also a fireplace just outside from the indoor bar area, yet still close-by to where I was at, making it sweet for an indoor/outdoor gathering of gals. If there was a chill in the air, of which later into the night could only serve to benefit me, I'm sure, the fireplace would be lit for the wives to hover around while lounging back on a double sofa. The wealthy always have the best appointments!

A single guy and all these teddies and wine. Even the husbands would eventually have to succumb to the understanding that certain things were out of my control, therefore couldn't be blamed for anything. After all, what would they do in my shoes? Even with the best of our abilities a serious variable is still left to chance.

The scene of liquid lingerie began to flow in. Luckily, I'm still in great shape, as my body was not behind a bar, more out in front and exposed beyond the norm. But to be fair, I had to accept the two-way street. I was outnumbered. Though not required to wear or un-wear something special, I was just asked to look good. That, I can do!

Making cocktails and pouring wine for the ladies up close and personal, chatting on topics near and far, they weren't shy at all, and it certainly wasn't a disadvantage to my visual senses. It was all in good fun, and I kept my demeanor solid throughout, as it's an important part of my reputation, so clients ring me up for the next gig. I work to gain more work, not lose work by losing control. The temptation was present, though . . .

It's always better to act a bit reserved but open, until after I've read the energies and moods of all the guests, than I simply adjust accordingly and ride the slipstream of the collective conscious in that five-hour window of time. When I'm there to serve and take good care, it's more important how others perceive me than how I perceive myself. But it's not as mechanical as it may all sound with the psychological end, not with my length of experience. I easily become the master of the flow, operating loosely tight, appearing and disappearing through the night.

I like to move around at a party when I get the chance, do some quick empties or plate pick-up for the kitchen, taking a couple bottles of wine at another go-round, but it usually doesn't make itself available until after the first couple bar rushes. It never fails that when I stand at the bar station for 15 minutes, no one will need a drink. I leave for 30 seconds, and get back to have two or three guests waiting for me at the bar. The random nature of it all.

It's one of those rare parties where there was less catered appetizer food because it was all women, no men. With both genders present, there's always more, because men normally eat more. This was a chance for the ladies to control and minimize the edible surroundings, as many were dieting. It was like "Get a small bite to eat at home, and then come to the party"

With myself, I always go to the diner and grab a bite to eat before I go to a party, so I don't have food on my mind at all. I'm too much of a comfort food animal, so half the fancy tray-passed mini-bites at events I really don't care for all that much, anyway. I do like the mini-quiche though, just don't call me Lorraine!

The ladies had a great time, and it was like *Project Pajama Runway* for me, so I could never complain. I got the opportunity to watch a bunch of gorgeous, married women for the most part, really let their hair down and be themselves, saying anything, with no men around. I felt a little gay on paper being so privy.

Debbie's husband got back to the house of logs sometime after midnight, maybe closer to one. The girls were in high uninhibited spirits even before then. Mark came over to me at the bar, smiled and said "So, how's it going?" I had a couple drinks at the guest's request, so I was feeling pretty good, but his expression made me crack up almost with a feeling of guilt as I poured him a glass of Red, but hadn't done anything questionable or crossed the line.

However, there's no doubt in my mind of the possibility of my presence being known between the wives and husbands either in advance or afterwards, could have been used as the chosen fantasy tease of the night when they got home, for the so-inclined, at no extra compensation for my bi-location services.

End of the night. I pack it all up, unload in the truck down below on the street, and have a smoke in the dark with the bright stars in the sky. With only a short gallop home, I take my time departing the neighborhood, because it's one of those beautiful, clean ranch-style communities, where you just don't want to leave. It brings back memories of the child in time.

8

USE YOUR ILLUSION

It was early 1991. I was just going about my day getting some errands done in the area and then onto a workout. I was living in Granada Hills at the time, several blocks away from the 405 freeway, in the valley. Soon after I returned to the house, I was going to kick back by the pool for a while, but I received a call from Tom at The Gardenia asking me to come in at 4:00pm instead of my usual 5:30pm arrival time.

I was told that a couple people were coming over from the Record Plant Recording Studios, and they just wanted to hang out at the bar and talk for a while during their break over a few drinks with the front doors still closed to the public, of which open at 7:00pm. I said "Sure, no problem" I got the call with just enough time in advance so I could still shower, get a bite to eat, and then get on the road into Hollywood.

The studios and the nightclub are maybe a long football throw apart from each other, separated by a mutual alley that is usually very walker-busy during both the day and night, and Sycamore Ave. Next door to The Gardenia was the plant nursery and a small film/television editing studio, which is now a guitar-making school. Off to the side of the alley about 30 yards south and between the club and the Record Plant is a fenced-in two-story building that houses the adult entertainment club known as The Zone. What a strange triangle these three night-based operations are, so close together, though the Plant is almost 24/7, as artists come in at all hours to record.

I get to the club at the requested time. I see Tom in the office, and he lets me know that Rose, the President of the Record Plant is coming over with a friend named Slash. I started laughing to myself a little bit realizing Tom was not as familiar with Slash as I was. At the rock nightclub I worked at in the late 80's just before The Gardenia, I remember the DJ playing several tracks from Guns N' Roses *Appetite for Destruction* album, as it was all the rage at the time with tons of radio play.

Well, this is cool. Not knowing the exact moment they were to be walking down the alley and knocking on the back door, I immediately started to get the bar ready and alive for the party of two. I didn't turn any low background music on, as I figured tunes were the last thing they wanted to hear, so I kept a quiet ambiance and left the option to them.

This type of thing had happened previously before I worked at the club, as I was told by Tom at a later time that Rose and Rod Stewart had come over. My guess was that Tom and Rose had gotten to know each other when he had the back outdoor patio open to walk-over lunches for the surrounding businesses during the early years just after he had got the place up and running.

At that time I had only been working at the club for maybe a year and a half, so my wild energy was still trying to adapt to this more civilized environment, even though I would still be in and out with the craziness of the packed LA club atmosphere. It was just something that I had to continue doing at the time.

With the ice up and the juices and fruit tray from the cooler, all I had to do was clear the clean glassware placed on the bar top that had come from the kitchen washer. The whole room was lit pretty dim, and I did about the same with the lights at the bar, kept it nice and comfortable. I heard Tom open the back door. They had arrived. At that moment, I looked to the liquor bottles in the back bar, searching for the Jack Daniels, as I knew what Slash's spirit of choice was.

"Fuck . . . you've gotta be kidding me", I said to myself. I'll be damned if we weren't out of Jack!

Rose and Slash came into the main room and over to the bar, taking the very back two seats closest to the wall. The three of us calmly introduced ourselves. They were there to take a load off for a while, so I matched the same energy, all the while still knowing I was out of the prized Tennessee sour mash, but not for long . . .

I made Rose a vodka/soda with lime. Slash asked me for a double-Jack on-the-rocks. Though I had Beam sitting back there, I didn't want him to settle for that. I said "Slash, I need to see if we have a bottle in the back room, I'll be right back". After lighting their cigarettes and quickly fetching them both a couple glasses of ice water, I disappeared for a few. Checking the liquor cabinet at light speed in Tom's office, no such luck! I said "Tom, I'll be right back. I have to do this".

I went out the back door running, and instead of jumping in my truck with shit-slow traffic, I ran down the alley to La Brea Blvd and caught the green light to cross Santa Monica Blvd. Blowing through the crosswalk and dashing the final 80 yards into the Thrifty Drug store (aptly-named!), I secure a bottle of the precious in my hands. Pacing like this, I try and calm my manic behavior as I'm in line two people back. This is when one of the two registers open decides to close, of course! This can't not happen . . .

I figured I'm still making good time, as long as both Rose and Slash decide to use the restroom while I'm missing in action. My power sprint back was now handicapped with a bottle in a bag that

I had to make sure not to drop while in the closing laps of the hurdle. It's good I had the right shoes on that gripped the pavement like a tiger paw, or I'd be ass over tea kettle in no time going this speed. That was back at the age of 32 when I could still run with the wolves. Today, I bicycle with the wolves!

Making it back with heat emanating from every pore, I try and put the calm back in my stride as I enter the back of the bar, not letting them know where I've just been. I grab a large tumbler glass, ice it up, proceed with the double-Jack in cool but minimal hand flair, and serve it with a spinning cocktail napkin to a smiling Slash. All better, back to normal, and to what it should have been.

About 30 minutes go by as I'm continuing my bar prep, which includes the cutting of the limes, lemons and oranges so the scent/zest of the skin oils enter the airspace and create a nice aroma in the small room, and Rose gets up to use the restroom. I guess my previous wish wasn't granted ! But it did give me a moment of time alone at the bar with Slash, almost too much undivided attention. I had to make any inquiry with no time to waste, as I was not to join in on their conversation together.

I chatted up the basic with him, then asked what he was working on over at the studio. He was cool and laid back, very articulate in his speaking, saying that he was laying down all the lead guitar parts to the new *Use Your Illusion I & II* albums, the highly-anticipated follow-up to the ground-breaking *Appetite* album. Both *Illusion* albums ended up being released on the same day in September of that year. At that time, not many people knew that it was going to be a double release of two separate-but-together albums of all-new original material. I felt privileged !

Rose returned, and from then on, I only paid attention to their drink levels, keeping up with fresh rounds at all times. They were there for a little over two hours catching up while knocking back a few, so after I finished the complete bar set-up and inventory, I left the room and went in back for a short while and talked with Tom and Andy the waiter, who had just arrived.

I never found out if Slash had just finished a long recording session, in the middle of one, or was about to begin an all-nighter. I'm sure it depends on if he prefers to jam and record at night or during the day. But when artists of this caliber and label-backing go into the studio, they're usually booked anywhere up to 12 hours at a time, or maybe more, which basically overlaps solar and lunar hours.

Not much has changed with the club or the studio since then. Both places are like long-standing institutions now. And yes, I'm still there too. Earlier this year, though, now exactly 20 years later, I asked Tom if Rose was still over at the studio. He hadn't heard any different so, I asked him if he would call her up to see if I can come over and take a quick tour of the legendary facilities. I got the green light sometime the following week and went in to meet Sayoko, the booking manager, doing the honor for me. It was an awesome experience, couldn't thank them enough.

Toward the end, Rose came downstairs and I was able to say hello again after not seeing her for so long. All that time and she still remembered me. Both of us have hardly changed. It's like this exact area of LA has an unknown time void surrounding it and no one ages, well, except for on the inside.

9

A SEASON INTERRUPTED

I remember it all pretty clearly, for good reason. I moved into the area of Woodland Hills in September of 93'. Four months later in January of 94', the Northridge Earthquake hit hard at 4:30am, just an hour after I laid down to go to sleep. The distance between the actual epicenter which was in Reseda (a town bordering Northridge), and my new digs was only 8 miles, which basically put us in the next to the last outer ring in the surrounding area of the San Fernando Valley.

It was aftershock city for weeks and months following, becoming a semi-perpetual state of emergency for some time before activity decreased. But with this type of natural disaster, there is no notice, making it a rough surprise when it's always around the corner. My old 50lb. Pioneer HPM100 speakers went flying across the room, almost kissing each other in the middle. Luckily, I didn't get clobbered. Outside, the same thing was happening as far as movement, with trees, trashcans, telephone poles, transformers and wires.

Many minor quakes on the Richter you can sleep through, but not this one. It was like a hand from the land of the giants grabbed the top and sides of the house, nearly shaking it off its foundation. It rocked hard for a good 20-30 seconds, then continued rolling for what must have been a couple minutes. Attention to time is a bit lost when you're instantly amped up with adrenaline. We were lucky on our particular block, as some houses in the area were wrecked, and needed major repairs to be lived in again.

The mutual fence in the backyard took a dive in the weak center, and I could see the neighbor's dog, Spanky, was alone and shaking. There was an open space of clearance in the fence's gaping wound, so I called the dog over. He hesitated for a moment, then with wagging tail he hopped through and slow-galloped over to me as I was sitting on the sundeck. We calmed each other down for close to an hour, than his owners got home. I walked him back over to the fence to meet his master, and back through he went.

For the rest of that year and more, with so much damage caused everywhere around, some $20 billion worth, where collapsed freeway sections took a serious chunk of that for repairs, and close to a dozen hospitals in the area had to be evacuated into other facilities, a disaster of this magnitude doesn't leave the mind very soon, another after-effect that takes time for you to begin to feel that you're back on somewhat solid ground again. Ten years gone and there were homes still getting repairs, almost in time for a next one!

The following year in April of 95', and I'm off work on a Saturday night. How weird! What am I going do with myself? I go play hoops for an hour and a half of pick-up games in the gym at the park over on Shoup Avenue, biking distance, but I don't take my bike. I'm paranoid enough just making sure my game-favored ball doesn't get lifted.

I get back to the house just in time, getting a call from Kelly at Café Bellissimo, the phone ringing as I walked in the door. Having only worked there for 8 months, she's frantic and busy while telling me she was in emergency need of a bartender due to a scheduling snafu. I had to be there in two hours, plenty of time considering all

I had to do was walk over and across Ventura Boulevard to the restaurant, the closest I've ever lived to a workplace.

I got pretty psyched for this event. Kelly tells me that the whole place is rented out for the night by the Los Angeles Dodgers to celebrate the 50th birthday of hitting and first base coach, Reggie Smith. A couple of the wives of players/coaches lived in the area and frequented the unique venue, with the entertainment being the entire singing server staff, so that was the connection in. The 95' season didn't get underway until April 25th, after the 94' season's player strike cut that year short with just 114 games played out of a 162-game schedule, so in total there were about 60 games lost.

Wow, I'm thinking "I can't wait to call Dad after I get back home", following the gig's end. My father is both an Angels and Dodgers fan, but he started with the Brooklyn Dodgers when he was younger living in New York, before I came around. In fact, my parents got married the year the Dodgers moved to Los Angeles, so when we finally moved out West in 1966, Dad felt much closer to his home team, but Anaheim (back when it was called The Big A) was a closer drive to ballgames, so we caught more of the American League.

The bar at Café B was more of a glorified service bar with a few seats around the corner. But it was really all I needed, and was used to knowing how to set it up for speed and efficiency, from the Black Angus days. I get in there and do a quick-basic inventory and started pulling the needed product from the backroom. With the glassware and backup ice in place, I was in a cockpit for cocktails !

The sedans and limos started arriving one-by-one, and within 30-40 minutes we were packed to the gills with players, coaches, and wives. Out of uniform, some players you can barely recognize without a name on the back of their shirt. But the starters stood out more clearly, players like Mike Piazza, Eric Karros, Raul

Mondesi, Delino DeShields, Jose Offerman, Hideo Nomo, Ramon Martinez, Todd Worrell, Tim Wallach, Pedro Astacio, Kevin Tapani, Chan Ho Park, Tom Candiotti, Ismael Valdez, as well as coaches Manny Mota and Bill Russell.

It wouldn't be a party though without manager Tommy Lasorda. A man of his stature arrives and it's like the game changes. He pretty much took the stage as the emcee for the night's festivities. I made drinks face-to-face at the bar for many of the players, and the waiters picked up drinks for their tables out in the main rooms.

I remember Eric Karros and his wife sitting down for dinner about 10 feet to my left, several were out on the large outdoor patio, and a surprise unexpected appearance, for me anyway, of Eric Davis, who took the whole year of 95' off to heal all of his injuries. He came to the bar and ordered a cocktail, and hung out for a couple minutes while getting a lay of the land.

I asked him about the status of the strike's end, and he mentioned that things were slowly getting sorted and settled but didn't know when a deal would be struck, but gave me a hint that it would be soon. When plans for replacement players was put on the table, that's when negotiations got serious, and soon after on April 25th, they resumed play with only missing a handful of games in the 95' season.

There was a lot of energy in the room, loud with musical interludes through the night from not only the waiters, but Kelly's husband-owner, Emilio, who got up and jammed a couple songs. He was a member of the 60's band *The Standells*. Tommy took the microphone for a speech or a story or three, and to talk about his friend and coach, Reggie Smith. With Italian food in the air and many bottles of vino leaving the wine racks for the tables, everyone was having a good time and getting their fill on.

The birthday cake was brought out from the coolers, and the entire crowd and staff including myself after a couple drinks, began singing Happy Birthday to Reggie, with Lasorda leading the way. It always feels good to get past the heavy rushes that I manage behind the bar, to where I can kind of drop my gear down a notch or two and relax a little bit, but you know, it never ends until it ends. The evening, however, went by all too fast. We wished all the players a great season, and the vehicles they own or rented, took them away like a shot in the night.

How odd this baseball-themed one-off gig, as just a few months later my friend Tony Jenkins, who operated many of the electronic flipping-Ad machines at major league sporting events, always sitting behind Nicholson at the Laker games at the Forum, doing the Clipper games at the Sports Arena, called me up and asked if I could make it down to San Diego on a certain date.

He was working the machines of the Padres vs. Reds series. I made it down there for the night, and both of us sat in the Reds dugout for the entire game with his laptop on his lap. Here I am hangin' on the bench with the likes of Barry Larkin, Ron Gant, Deion Sanders, Bret Boone, Hal Morris, Reggie Sanders, Benito Santiago, Mariano Duncan, Jose Rijo, and David Wells, to name a few of the notables. Also there was coach, Hal McRae, and manager, Davey Johnson.

The whole time I kept my mouth shut, while chewing tobacco and sunflower seeds ruled the floor and a few holed-out cans. I felt like a teenager again eating popcorn down there, but fuck it I was hungry, being the same age if not older than some of the players. In back of the dugout you're basically under the stands. Tony would tell me that during some games where he worked close by the players, a few would go in back here and there and talk shop, get a bite to eat from the buffet, have a smoke or whatever, mainly just getting out of the limelight for a few short moments. I said to Tony "They smoke cigarettes?" He says "Yeah, just a couple of them, but they're already dipping, so what's the difference!"

The Dodgers and Reds ended up taking first place in their respective divisions, and met in the playoffs, where the Reds swept them 3-0 in a 5-game series, with the first two games being at Dodger Stadium.

To come sort of full circle so many years later, that just a year and two years ago, I got the call to work the bar for a couple of private parties at the home of Mike Scioscia, the manager of the Angels, my Dad's other favorite team. That'll be another story for down the road.

Baseball has always been close to my heart, from all of the Padres exhibition games I went to as a 10-12 year old kid living in Yuma, AZ, hanging out with the players, the country-singing star Charley Pride, watching Warren Spahn pitch a couple innings, and being introduced to famous announcer Dick Enberg, has all led up to these events of the past, and the present.

The people I've been fortunate enough and in a position to meet, have always been my constant source of inspiration.

10

REACH THE BEACH

A Highway Patrol car U-turns while I stretch the distance out to a hundred yards or more going the opposite direction, a matter of seconds and the lights rapidly getting closer. I slow down, pull over and surrender. For the first time in 10-15 years, I get a ticket. Exceeding the speed limit, guilty as charged ! I wasn't even in a hurry to get to my gig.

Cruising early on the road with my iced chocolate coffee from Michael D's Diner and listening to Candlebox on the Pioneer, I accidentally exit the third tunnel on Kanan/Dume Road going towards the water like a hot wheel kicked out of a super charger. That part of the tunnel and continued road that leads to PCH begins the long descent back to lower ground, and I just missed cooling the jets down on my own by three seconds at the time the officer noticed my pace.

I had all kinds of bar kit accessories both in the passenger seat and in the open back of the truck. He was curious when he approached the window slowly. Strangely enough, he guessed what it was after taking a short look-see. Thankfully, there was no digging around, as my filled vermouth atomizers were deep in the pack. How would I go about explaining to him the 99% truth that vermouth isn't the type of spirit that one really drinks straight ?

After some reasoning with the officer as to why, and taking his finger-eye test to prove to him that I wasn't high in any way, I catch a serious break on the citation. I was in the wrong, but he understood as to why it could momentarily happen on that area of road where, with no other cars in front of you for a half-mile or more, it catches you at the start of it, and you have to slowly re-adjust the speed down accordingly to avoid any rubber burn on the asphalt.

I absorb the semi-costly 15-minute pause, and moved forward with my day of duty, happily escaping worse.

Making a right turn onto PCH, I shag it all the way out to where the old Trancas Nightclub used to be, as directly across the street on the South side of the highway was my work destination, the Malibu West Beach Club. It sits between Zuma State Beach and Broad Beach, not too far from The Colony, an area overall where many celebrities have lived secluded through the decades.

At the nearby Carbon Beach is the famous *Deal Maker's Rock*, where all the heads of studios meet, exercise and walk in the morning, and make their movie deals. But whether this happens as much now as it did back in the day is anybody's guess, though I'm sure the rock still remains.

MWBC is one of my favorite venues to work. I've been behind the bar for many weddings here, always setting up stage on the outside deck overlooking for hours of stunningly beautiful views of the Pacific Ocean during the day and night. On a clear afternoon, Catalina Island and the Channel Islands even come into focus at a yonder.

Including the interior clubhouse and patio, the place holds about 120 comfortably, though they claim a higher occupancy number.

It's possible to cram more in, I suppose, but not without hindering the floor staffs' ability in the dining room to move quickly in and out of the 10-person table rounds without bumping and dumping plates and stemware on shirts and dresses, not to mention the levels of guest movement throughout the evening needing to be of ease as well. A lot of this happens just out of the mere fact that the dance floor is placed more in the middle than off to one side or another.

I'm always thankful of having my own space to work within behind the bar, keeping *oops* to a minimum. There's enough to watch out for in my safe haven of constant drink activity, and as the initial guest-greeter for the night's festivities post-ceremony. But as a keen observer, I can see everything else going on too. You develop a knack to just know where to look after awhile.

I park close and unload all my gear, lugging it in three different trips up the steps and through the main room to the outer back deck where the wedding ceremony takes place. I like getting there before anyone else so I can grab a clean start. There can be a lot to do, especially with the use of real glassware, and half the time I don't know if things will be set up or not when I arrive, so I have to go with the notion of scratch instead of expectation. There are banquet tables to the side and back of the bar which gives a lot of efficient placement space for product usage, along with some spirit brand showcasing, but if the bar is set up on the other side of the deck it can be too tight for comfort and speed, with less square footage made available.

Initially, the guest seating for the ceremony is lined up in several rows out on the open deck, so in the early goings, there's some floor shape-shifting that goes on immediately following the exchange of vows, where the chairs used outside have to go back inside and placed around the tables for seating and dining. This happens at the exact moment where I'm buried in a beverage-parched bull rush at the bar with cocktails and champagne flowing, as most of the time alcohol is not served before the ceremony at the request of the bride, groom, and families. It was juices, waters, and sodas *only* at the beginning.

Guests that are now facing me several deep barely even notice it happening, the chair transport getting completed in less than five minutes, and all the sudden the outer deck is wide-open space to walk around and hang out in for the rest of the evening, with a few tall cocktail table rounds linen-dressed and spread about.

Even on a cloudy day or night, the place is still a beautiful setting no matter what. The bride and groom are married with the Pacific Ocean as a backdrop. With the water only a hundred yards out, it's hard to find a better (or closer) venue than this for both a wedding and reception party combined under one roof. And when it's clear blue skies with a warm/cool breeze and a gorgeous full moon in the night above, it becomes unbeatable. Many celebrities have also been married here from what I've heard, but that info is kept on the hush, though I do know that Traci Lords was married there in 2002.

It's not just a place where people get hitched, though. They book it out to whomever wants to use and pay for the facility, so various parties, class reunions, anniversaries, auction-fundraisers, corporate events, and film location managers take advantage of this unique, yet unassuming two-story structure just a barefoot walk on white sands to the breaking surf, complete with a Baywatch-style lifeguard tower, and dolphins leaping out of the water as they swim by.

All the gigs I've worked here have been through Pierre's Catering out of Westlake Village. I've been on-call with him for about 5 years now. Pierre has his own unique personality that one has to get used to. He's loose, happy, a little wild, and an exciting face on the floor, which is a good thing in my book. It's a lot better that way than a catering owner or manager putting all the floor staff on pins and needles, of which I've dealt with before working with previous outfits, so I notice the difference in energy. In my opinion, the less catering snobbery in the business, the better for everyone involved, including the guests.

We've had a good and understanding professional relationship, and work well together, but it took a little while for us to get our wires in sync. He also has a sizeable staff of people that have been with him for a long time, which makes my tenure so far always looking like the new kid on the block.

Both Pierre and I have a lot of energy on-location. We like to work in advance of the game, arriving two hours+ beforehand. It helps to be ahead of things when there's so much timing to consider, as events of this nature and at a rented facility have both a start time and an end time. You can imagine what goes on in-between!

The chaos at different stages and intervals can drive anybody nuts once in a while, but the more experience you have doing this one-off occasion sort of thing, the more you just let it roll off and move on with the always-evolving chores at hand. Otherwise, in can all too easily turn into a shift of temporary angers and muted frustrations.

I remember two years ago a couple who lived in New York City who were getting married there, as I was notified by Pierre to get in contact with them about new, creative cocktail selections they wanted to come up with for the bar. A month before the wedding, the bride and I must have went back and forth 10 or more times each on email. She was nice in thinking she had a handle on the mixology world, suggesting this and that craft-style cocktail from bars or mags, which is all fine with me as I've done several party drink menus, but her choices were lacking a clearer direction and purpose with what people like to drink from the east coast to the west coast, given its climate differences and season at hand.

Though several guests were flying out to L.A. for the occasion, the far majority attending actually lived here, which had to be taken into strong consideration over the need of the New York ego bleeding to impress others. We settled on a Superfruit Fizz, Minted Gin Rickey, Peach-Pomegranate Margarita, and a seasonal drink of mine called Pink Floyd, which was quite the hit, and tastes so good even I drink it! Once I helped her understand the specific set of time-infused particulars vs. body count involved and somewhat reduced capabilities with an outdoor portable scratch bar as opposed to the fully-operational, cooler-stored bar establishment that was in her mind's eye, than we finally made it onto the same page.

I'm such a journeyman at this place and time in my 30-year career behind the bar, that nothing fazes me anymore. At times, it's almost an out-of-body experience. Am I really here doing this work for the thousanteenth time? I'm like a Grandpa in the bar business and I'm only 52, yet I look about 38. But regardless of my stellar credentials, I still plow through like a high-powered bar warrior, with my usual charm, kindness, and youthful look and exuberance getting into the spirit and energy of the party, once again. It's like I never left . . .

In my position, I have to be one with the people/guests. They feel more comfortable in knowing that I'm not just going to be some stale, mindless drink robot going through the motions with short, dry communication for them, get paid then go home. There's more to it than that for me. Bartending is rarely looked at as performance art, but in many ways that's exactly what it is, and one can also create it as such, from simple to complex culinary skills with the spirit and liquid arts.

This is what I've accomplished over the years, a state of *Barisma*, bringing the right personality, level of electricity, and style of magnetism to the bar, along with an organized *mise en place* creating quick, agile physical movements in a continuous fluid motion of icing, pouring, cutting, muddling, squeezing, juicing, zesting, shaking and garnishing with just the right amount of minimal flare technique in the middle of it all, both the mental and physical operating as one.

At a wedding I worked at MWBC a little over a year ago, this guy comes up to me at the bar. We looked at each other and said hello, he recognizes me, but I suffer the silent lapse in return. It was Chris Young, who I used to rock with behind the bar from 85'-87' at the Black Angus in Burbank during those busy days when the nightclub end of the chain was promoted at its peak. We hadn't seen each other in over 20 years. Chris wasn't married then, but he's married now! He still looked like he could be the late Dan Fogelberg's brother.

It was great to catch up with him during the rare slow spots of the night. He's been out of the bar game for most of that whole time gone, but Chris was vital early on for teaching me the pace of high-volume when I was struggling into the gear with how fast I needed to move. I was built-for-speed, but felt like a turtle coming out of the gates compared to his end-of-shift ring totals. Then I caught up . . .

Being present as a single man behind the bar at so many weddings over the last 10 years, it still hasn't warmed me up to the idea of actually going through with it myself. It's been an interesting detachment for me as something I don't crave, although I completely enjoy watching it all happen for others, a short distance away, with drinks ready. This is the closest I get to saying "I Do", by hearing it! So near, and yet so far away . . .

The looks from a few single ladies eventually gravitate to the bar after a drink or two, wondering if I have a significant other. It's happened many times before. They don't have to verbalize it. I can see it in their eyes. But they should know better than to marry a bartender or someone in a position who works crazy hours of the night, unless they're doing the same. On the surface of the job, it all looks good and cool and sexy, but the other side of the life would be burdened by on-call difficulties and early weekend mornings when I hit the sack. It's the opposite of a 9 to 5.

Beyond that, they need a deep sense of trust in knowing that I won't be banging any female strangers at the bar. I don't need my spouse conducting a private investigation on me, which has happened in the past, and won't happen again, not after I proved my discipline to be even stronger than hers.

At the end of the night, we're all pretty much spent with the energies dispensed to pull off another event without a hitch. The clean-up and load-up is always the last thing for us to do, and the last thing we want to do. Pierre's vans back-up so we can all lend a hand, though I have my own shit to lug back out as well, from a little farther away. I try to keep occupied doing a little bit of both, so I'm not always the last staffer to leave. Like other outfits I work with, we become a catering caravan.

Apron off, shirt off, fleece coat on, the finish line gets a big breath of completion. Heading back up through Kanan/Dume on the way home to the valley, I light up a long-awaited smoke and watch my speed, listening to Coast to Coast KFI-AM 640 – More Stimulating Talk Radio . . .

Last year in 2012 was the 50-year anniversary of this private beachfront club. Check it out! Website – www.malibuwestbc.com

Pierre's Catering – www.pierrecatering.com

Always a pleasure to pour here, looking forward to the next time in Malibu.

Surf's Up !

11

PSYCHEDELIC NIGHT

One of my rare occasional clients is a V.P. at Bank of America. She lives out in Newberry Park, a 25-minute drive off the 23 Freeway which slices between the 101 and the 118, basically in the Ventura County. I love going the opposite direction for a gig instead of always having to hop into the heart of L.A.

Mary was celebrating her 60th birthday in 2009 with a 60's themed cocktail party at her home, and wanted to know if I was available when she called and left a message on my cell. It had been so long, I almost forgot who she was. I'm glad I wasn't near my phone, or I may have well embarrassed myself by answering it with a blank slate in my head. Who are you again? I've had so many gigs in so many places around L.A. year after year in the last decade, it's impossible to keep track of them all.

However, after listening to her message, it was her beautifully smooth voice and slightly Southern accent that made me remember her as clear as day. Something about women from the South that just takes my cake. It doesn't hurt that she is a very attractive 60 as well! Checking my calendar, I was relieved that she chose the only Saturday I had open in the following month of October, week 2.

I called her back in the early evening and we started talking about the party particulars. She was going all out with a band and food catered, with a guest count of about 60. I knew she needed a bar, so this time I let her know I had my own custom bar. This put more money in my pocket and allowed her to skip having a cheap portable delivered from a rental outfit, which most of the time I can't stand to work out of with the functional *mise en place* extremely limited, always having to modify to the gills with my own side gear in order to make it through the night with a smile still remaining on my face.

Many home parties I'm working out of very nice built-in bars, but with rentals you never quite know what's going to be there when you show up. My prayers sometimes help when I'm en route to mystery gigs, but there have been some very short-sighted clients in the past, where I arrive and think to myself "Oh my god, you've got to be kidding me. You want me to operate efficiently out of this with how many guests?"

Luckily I've been able to train clients over the years to have what I need, not what they think is mildly sufficient enough to get by with. The rich can be such cheap asses sometimes, it's unbelievable to witness right there in the moment staring at them. Sucking it up with a total shit bar set-up has never been the best practice for me. Some steam is bound to exit my eye sockets in the early stages.

But I have my own bar now to buffer problematic situations. I need to look good doing my work. I highlight and entertain the guests. That's what I do, and I do it well, so the stage needs be lit accordingly, or I'm going to struggle through a faulty performance. Working in real operational bars for the first 20 years of my career (and still do on-call at The Gardenia Room), I dealt with similar function issues, but those fixtures are more permanent than mobile, yet still can make the work behind any bar a bit miserable shift-after-shift. Unless of course, I get bong high on some good, sticky bud and down a couple shots to the point where my concern and interest for excellence diminishes, then it'll be like, whatever! I prefer to always give my best, though, straight – no chaser . . .

We confirmed and booked, and I emailed her my full dry and wet stock beverage list as a guideline for her bar purchases, letting her also know that I would bring the ice with me, which is always a nice convenience for the client. But they are responsible for the booze, to alleviate any liability on my end.

The few weeks went by in a flash with other numerous gigs completed, and I pulled up to the street in front of her home at 5:00pm for a 7:00pm start. Bringing the whole bar and kit thing takes me more time to set-up with the extra schlepping and assembly. At the same time the musicians in the band show up in staggered arrivals, bringing their gear in as well, setting up in another sizeable part of the house near the backyard screen door.

Mary and I decided to turn the living room into the entire bar area to help spread things out and avoid guest-clog. I had a good space with everything I needed – top, under bar and back table. Designing a creative, fun bar theatre for everyone comes from the thrill of being clever and the enjoyment to assist the entertainment.

With all the decorations that Mary and her friends put up all through the home during the day, I felt like I walked right into a 60's/70's show, with love beads everywhere! We covered the black linen-draped front of the bar with vinyl peel-and-stick decals of peace signs, yin and yang signs, smiley faces, free love, summer of 69', and whatever else was in the bag. It looked very cool, man!

I had all my black and black on below the waist for comfort and flexibility, but I wore a cool tie-dye shirt with a black vest to show above the bar top. I fit into the theme very easily, as I was a child of the 60's and a teen in the 70's, being part of what it was all about – Freedom. The only thing missing was my normally long, wavy hair. But I wasn't about to throw an unfitting wig on. Though appropriate, it's weird-feeling and causes funky perspiration when I'm moving and shaking for many hours into the night.

After stocking the bar with all the essential beverage needs and then some, I still went over and raided Mary's liquor stash in one of the kitchen cabinets to see if there were a few extra things I could play with behind the bar to kind of round-out the capabilities. At many parties over the years, I've always created new drinks in the moment with whatever I can put together in a chemist sort-of way.

Even though this was the hippie counter-culture side of Mad Men, I still made a few cocktails of the period like the Classic Martini, the Old Fashioned, and the Cuba Libre. I brought my signature Peanut M&M's and sugar-dusted Lemon Heads once again adding to the bars' garnish and buffet selection. Like a hunter spotting a dear, the M&M's are always the popular highlight to get drained the earliest, refilling often. But it was hard to compete with the 60's candy that Mary had on hand, including Pixy Stix, Razzles, Sweet Tarts, 100 Grand Bars, even Candy Cigarettes and Scooter Pies.

The dinner food was also a great choice, catered in by Wood Ranch Barbeque out of Agoura Hills, one of my favorite places to munch. I feel like I'm out on the range with good staple and comfort food like that. I could drink their barbeque sauce!

The set-up and prep went by in its usual "where'd the time go" speed, and before you knew it, we were off and running. Guests were arriving in two's and three's and soon I was in that rush mode of keeping up pace with demand and supply to crank through the first of many drink waves, something I'm all too familiar with. Thankfully it's more of a cruise now instead of a constant stress, but that's the beneficial change that occurs when you stay ahead of the pressure. And wanting to kick ass with the speed and flair of a sport certainly helps sustain the mood, along with everyone else's.

It didn't take long before all of us became a bunch of peace frogs after some drinks and the quality herb of today faintly swirling around in the air. I was mildly theme-dressed compared to the partygoers who came in the most amazing costumes, bringing back a lot of hilarious bell-bottom memories. The band was jamming all these incredible songs from Jefferson Airplane, The Doors, Janis Joplin, Hendrix, The Beatles, The Kinks, Cream, The Yardbirds, Traffic, The Beach Boys, The Stones, Bob Dylan, The Who, and of course The Grateful Dead, many more.

During the latter breaks between their many sets of the evening, the band members would all come over to the bar once they had warmed up, and had some drinks to enhance the groove they set for themselves. Overhearing and participating in their conversations at their interest, I soon found out that these players were all session and studio musicians. No wonder they rocked the songs. They knew them inside out, being of the age. However, it's kind of sad to me that such talent ends up playing house parties, but that's part of the struggle with being an artist of any kind, you take what's available. Through the Local 47 Musicians Union, they gig all over L.A. much in the same way that I do.

The female keyboardist and vocalist was a two-tour side player with Jimmy Buffett, and the bass player was a member of Ricky Nelson's Stone Canyon Band for 8 years. Sitting closest to the bar, he mentioned to me and a couple others unknowing, that he left the band only one year before the tragic plane crash and fire on New Year's Eve in 1985 that was en route from Alabama to Dallas, Texas, killing everyone onboard except for the two pilots. Lucky man! He said he still has an original packet of guitar picks saying "Stone Canyon Band" on them. Now that's eerie . . .

In fact, just earlier last year in January, Ricky's brother, David passed away in Century City at the age of 75. Harriet died in 1994 in Laguna Beach, and Ozzie died in 1975 in Hollywood.

At midnight, the birthday cake was brought out and all of us got together to sing Happy Birthday. Mary's a wonderful lady and a lot of fun to be around. She had a great time, and was also smart enough to have a couple friends hanging out on stand-by to tackle the majority of clean-up when it came time.

The party kicked on till about 1:00am before I began the bar's trimming of the sails. There's always the time when festivities have to come to an end, but we never really want them too. There is no barback with my private gigs. I do everything myself – the set-up, the event's long middle passage, and the breakdown. Handling it all can be exhausting.

And then I get home and collapse . . .

12

COCKTAILS AND CLOTHING

In the late Summer/early Fall of 2005, I head out North all the way down Topanga Canyon Blvd. toward the 118 Freeway to Liquid Catering over in Chatsworth. My truck gets loaded down with product and ice, as Steve had me on an event in Hollywood where I had to be there at 4:00 pm. The gig was a designer jean sale party put on by the Canadian identical twin brothers, Chip & Pepper Foster, set in a big warehouse on Sunset Blvd., just a block east of the Hollywood Palladium.

The worst part with this type of delivery and bar job at times is getting too sweaty from load work before you even get yourself situated behind the bar with fresh composure. Mentally, you're changing gears from schlep to cheer, going from lift-labor power to smile, greet and pour energy. The dolly helped, but can't we just hire a barback who will gladly do this shit so we can stay more on point with our own job description? I checked in with the other two bartenders that Steve had on for the night, and we split up the early duties after the heavy moving of 50lb. ice bags were all in and tubbed.

Bacardi was sponsoring the bars, and their P.R. person, Laura Baddish, was my primary contact. She had flown in from New

York to be a part of the denim shindig and to make sure all goes off as planned with product placement across the bar tops. We had a few specialty drinks to make with a variety of spirits, but other than that it was beer, wine and champagne. We knew going into a 6:00pm start that we could be rolling hard if the place got packed, as hundreds of people were invited. It all depended on who shows up and the stagger in which they all arrive. Chip & Pepper had quite a following, and this was in the heart of Hollywood, so anything could happen.

I was thankful the 18-foot drink stage was raised to proper bar height, or it would have been brutal on the neck. Head down with crotch-view of the bartenders is not the most attractive presentation package to offer the guests, yet it doesn't stop the various cocktail competitions around the globe to suffer from this obvious lack of advance thought. But it's usually the hotel or venue that fails to supply the lift sticks with the stretch of banquet tables used. But I digress . . .

Racks of pants filled the numerous aisles in the center of the floor space with name cuts like Stella, Slider, Bump Watch, Ike Nifus, Bobby Baby, Bronson, Yellowknife, Kesha, Union Square, Renner, and Illinois from sizes 24-32 all going for generous discounts from their normal retail prices. I'm so relieved to be past the need for peer image with expensive, trendy brand clothing, a racket that the "in-crowd" people follow like sheep. The one benefit from this type of gathering is getting rid of a shitload of inventory overstock. The cool and safe precaution of invitation count avoids a potential injury stampede if it were to be heavily announced as open to the public, however more the hangers would have emptied.

The guys weren't hurting for money so, no desperation or liquidation sale here. It was all in fun, tied-in with a level of continued brand exposure and the media sources interested in covering it. Chip and Pepper were in the house to speak in the camera eye about the evening's festivities, as well as meet-and-greets, hanging with their invited friends, celebrity or otherwise (including Jenny McCarthy who I scoped when walking by) and eventually making it over to the bar for momentary chat over cocktails with us bartenders before another onslaught of interruptions. This is why we keep the conversations short and sweet at events like this. No time for depth or detail. Above all, Chip and Pepper are businessmen, but they also know how to have fun with their freedom, popularity and product line, so that respect always has to be kept in mind. Who wouldn't want to be in their position?

I'm such a simple-living guy when it comes to being in the middle of all the many gatherings I'm hired at. It's only my world when I'm behind the bar, but nothing I gravitate to in real life. When you realize how much hype there is behind everything of this nature, I just step back and let the pressure go by. I have no agenda. I have no investment. It's just my job and I do it well, staying out of the line of fire. Even with the news and indie cameras pointed in our faces at the bar with our black-colored Bacardi button-down shirts on, we just continue to do our thing. I still have the shirt today, sleeping in the closet with the rest of them from events past.

In the midst of the peak-volume hours of the night, I was trying with time-efficient purpose for five minutes or less of uninterrupted PR talk with Laura about a creative project proposal I had in mind. So much for no agenda! But the idea really didn't even hit me until after I was on-site for a while, always thinking on my feet. What Laura didn't know was that a couple years previous I had made contact via query letter with a high executive of Bacardi at their main headquarters on Pennsylvania Avenue in Washington D.C. (District of Criminals), after seeing his name and picture in an industry magazine.

That initial idea was to have the brand and their portfolio of other spirits to utilize any and many of my various-spirited cocktail preparations from my two DVD's with their marketing department, which also could have worked in creating a branded video disc in some of their holiday packaging instead of just some cocktail glass, the boring norm for many brands across the board. He actually sent me a reply letter some weeks after saying that he liked the idea a great deal, and asked that I send a media package to Steve Messer at Bacardi in Miami.

That was motivating news, considering an industry juggernaut like Bacardi would rarely take the time and awareness close to ten years ago to consider a creative from a lowly bartender way down on the chain that just happened to come up with another great promotional idea. And with the rare response I received, it basically meant that it was something they never thought of themselves, hard for the suits to admit when they always want it to be their idea, part of the beg, borrow and steal design they use to move up the ladder. Sometimes you have to go all the way to the top in order to get to the middle!

My wide range and variety of over 100 cocktail preparations that we shot in 2001 were the first-ever to be on the new DVD format at the time, with the debut DVD released when Blockbuster was still renting VHS movies on their shelves just before the slow shift-over began. Steve then asked that I send an identical media package to Laura at The Baddish Group at her offices on Seventh Avenue in New York. And so I did. I continued to make contact with Florida throughout the next year but, it eventually hit the brick wall of college-educated office people with no field or beverage experience, much less creative drive, and heard nothing back from Laura and her firm. I scratched their back but they didn't scratch mine. I could have developed many things for them, but the videos were too ahead of its time for them to grasp the significance. Too bad I couldn't have just stayed at the top. Today, brands are paying much more attention to the bartender world, finally recognizing that it's our hands their bottles are in, and what we could do with them.

Later in the night as things were on a slow fade, I took a short break and walked out to my truck to make sure it was still there. It was parked in the same spot on the side but near the entrance where I did the early drop and load. Security was hanging nearby so I needn't any worry. They had given me the okay to keep it there but, you know, things can change without prior notice. I have a quick smoke outside chatting with the uniform man while catching some fresh air. Well, fresh for L.A.!

Walking back inside, I notice Laura over to the far end of the bar, so I mosey on over and start-up my new proposal. They're not afraid to grow and expand in a big way, which intrigued me in hopes of working with them with stronger connections to consumers with drinks, especially when you know Bacardi's wild history with Cuba. And may possibly be the reason for the continued embargo the U.S. has on the island country in the Caribbean, to keep Havana Club rum out of the states. Imagine the number of lobbyists employed by the brand. Of course that doesn't keep the rich and entitled from smuggling Cuban cigars into the U.S. in their Diplomatic briefcases that are immune from being checked at Customs.

Keep in mind this was now only a year after Bacardi had purchased Grey Goose for $2.2 Billion from Sidney Frank. Four years later in 2008 I would be in France on a journalist tour, and we're driving through the countryside, I look to my left and there's Grey Goose, nothing more than a massive tin shed, and Sidney profits $1.6 Billion from the sale. Is the vodka really that good? I know the bottling is, which probably costs more if not as much to produce as the contents inside. But it's not the product value, it's the brand . . .

My idea with Laura was to fly over and visit the distilleries from all the brands under their umbrella to conduct individual video tours along with interviews with the master distillers in regards to processes and so forth, and treks out to the sugar cane fields or whatever to put together nice visual media pieces for them to use in a variety of ways, which could also include a few of my drink preparations in each. I had my videographer, Drew Rosenfeld, ready and willing, and I would be the on-camera host, since I had some pretty good experience at the time. Just a year before, we had shot and produced our beverage travel show pilot, Liquid Kitchen, so we had it down enough.

This project was simple, low overhead, and effective. Drew had his own post-production facilities, so we were ready to roll. Laura really liked the idea and said she would give it some thought and get back with me after she got back to her offices back east. I gave her my business card, and we left it at that, short and quick, so I could get back to the business at the bar.

We had one long last rush with cocktails before the evening sale would come to a successful close. Final appetizers of food were being passed, so we grabbed what we could devour while beginning the breakdown and pack-up of the bar's leftover stock, as I had to take it back to Liquid Catering on my way home. I get to the finish point of that, about ready to take off after a shirt change, and Laura comes walking out with an armload of jeans. She asks me to take them with me and have Steve, the owner of Liquid, package and send them back to New York for her, as she didn't have enough room in her suitcases. I'm sure this is something that Steve has never had to do for anyone before, so I glance at her with a bit of question in my eyes and proceed with the normal gestures of kindness and acceptance, since she heard my proposal out and all, but her and Steve had worked together on many L.A. events in the past, so I left it at that.

I get back to the warehouse and begin the beverage extraction from the truck, and Steve walks up. He gives me a hand with the boxes, and I mention there's something in the cab I need to retrieve. I hand him Laura's denim pile with her request, and he looks at me with the same look I gave her, but longer. I shook my head not knowing what to think of it myself, caught in the middle of something I'd rather be left out of. He realized I wasn't the creator of this, so he cut me loose. I'm sure he added the shipping and handling charge into the total balance of the bill.

Laura never got back in touch with me, again, the second time now whether she remembered or not. However, at some point in time after, I started getting these emails and calls from interns of her PR firm. This told me that she had taken the time to put me on her database for useless bullshit information, content and requests that I could do nothing with, making her office people look like total idiots when talking to someone with my bar background and experience in the industry, of which their poor public relations showed no bridge of understanding with cocktails, that which I tried to move forward with them in a good way.

It just felt like a nose was turned up at me for no good reason in return. It's unfortunate when simpatico ends empty, as there was so much to give and work with for the good of the industry. The arrogance of the New York ego strikes again! But the joke's on her because, I'm originally from upstate New York! A lack of due diligence on her part. Not to mention that I had been writing for the industry magazines for a few years at that time, including a regular monthly cocktail column called Liquid Kitchen, so it's not like I was lacking any proper exposure in the field. There was plenty of productive trust and faith to be gained from my fertile, creative ground.

In hindsight, they had little or no foresight into the media future, or so it reflected anyway. Innovation is not what they do best. They're more followers than leaders, though they want you to think otherwise. But what they really do is wait and sit back to watch direction, than navigate through already proven channels to avoid any risk or damage, and profit from someone else's idea.

Later that year and in 2006, YouTube launched, and the rest is history . . .

Since then, I sold my Liquid Kitchen.com internet/web domain to Kathy Casey Food (and Drink) Studios in Seattle so she could do her thing with it, and Drew Rosenfeld has been Senior Creative Director and Head of Production for Larry Flynt Productions in

Beverly Hills. I should give Drew a call sometime, haven't spoken to him in quite a while. Maybe we can do a porn drink show and call it CSI: Cocktail Scene Investigation. Just kidding, kind of . . (-;

13

A Danger Unforeseen

It was late August, 2005. I had just got home from a gig with Liquid Catering out in the West Hills/Bell Canyon area off of Valley Circle, in a sizeable recreation hall within a gated community. It was a memorial get-together for a teenage boy who had tragically lost his life. The night before at another gig, I felt good, but this day my energy didn't seem to rebound much at all from my normal sleep.

We had a perfect built-in bar set-up to work out of, so the unloading, stocking and ice drop all prepped as planned. I was working alongside Greg, another bartender from Liquid as well, so it was one of those gigs where 1½ bartenders would have been just right, leaving us sharing a few repeated breaks. Fine with me! Same pay, who cares? Greg was moving to Las Vegas the very next day, so his mind was both home and abroad. Myself, I just dial it in once in a while on an easy one. You can't be perfect every night, so I don't make an issue of it.

The theme of the event was best for us to be numb and humble, anyway, more like cocktail caretakers for the night, where facial expression and nodding the complemented visual lip read in a quietude of observance over alcohol, a rec. room for sorrow and buffet. Given my flat energy for the day, it was fitting for the mourners. I always store some reserve power within my armor in case of need, so I can hit the booster to crank it up whenever, but even that wasn't working tonight. Something was wrong. I had never felt an overall central drop in my physiological circuitry like this before. Even more curious, there was no reason for it at all.

I took a break, grabbed a small bite to eat, and sat down watching Greg pour in eye-shot off to the side in the back. Sitting ended up being a good and a bad thing to do. After 15 minutes, it felt like I had taken a couple valium. My food consumption was a scene in slow motion till the plate emptied. Of course, it was my time to take the bar now! My breathing became laboriously deeper out of necessity. Strange that it didn't feel like I was coming down with anything, as once every week or ten days I pop a tincture combination of Echinacea and Goldenseal to keep my immune system up and away from the common cold and flu, since we're always around and in contact with so many different people all of the time. Don't want to be tending bar with the sniffles, sore throats and congested coughs. Yuk!

We load and go home. My place at that time on the valley's old El Escorpion Road was only a few minutes away with no freeway, and I had the next couple days off to hopefully rest and regain. I get to bed well after midnight as usual after checking emails and watching a late movie over some well-stocked soup with organic vegetables. Everything was basically fine, but the fatigue was weird. I crashed with the window cracked just a bit for some fresh air to seep in.

Rising from the dead a little before Noon, I get out of bed and slowly attempt to stand up, but my knees buckled and I hit the carpet. A scary moment of unknown origin became urgent. I rarely ever have to go to the doctor. My medical life has always been about getting clobbered with major illnesses, while avoiding all the small stuff. The last big problem I had with a body issue was 8 years previous. I guess something was due, almost coming to expecting it.

I was parched like I've never experienced before, as though I hadn't drank any water in a month. I had no fucking clue what was happening, but I knew at this point I had to pick up the phone, if I could get to it! I sucked down a quart of water like I had been stranded in the desert, soaking my throat enough to speak to a receptionist. My doctor, Paul, at his office in the West Hills Medical Plaza, got me in at mid-afternoon, luckily catching him on one of the three days a week he's there. The final visual shocker was right before I hopped in the truck. All that water, and more following quart one, made me piss like a horse. But it came out brown in color. Uh oh! I stood in silent disbelief, praying it was an easy cure and go-away.

They call me in from the waiting room. Paul arrives 10-15 minutes later, looks at me, and my eyes, and says "I hope it isn't what I think it is". Great, that's all I need to hear. I give a urine sample, as that was ready to flow again, and the nurse takes my blood. I sit in a chair with complete emptiness of power, like someone disengaged the battery cables without my prior approval. I had no pain whatsoever, but the oncoming suffering of deprivation was now taking full control, but for how long?

With Paul at my side again, he offered up the dirty detail. Though we had to wait a day or two for the blood tests to come back, the worst case scenario was to hold true, though not yet confirmed. I had contracted Hepatitis A, from somewhere! I was livid inside, but I was too tired to show it. However, while waiting for the final blood results, the third day after I felt great. My energy bounced back. I was thinking they were wrong. On my way to work at the club, I get a surprise call on my cell from the L.A. County Health Department. They caught me just in time. She confirmed it over the phone with me. I said "Are you sure, because I feel fine now". She said "Yes, no doubt". At that point, I realized it was highly unsafe for me to work or be near anyone, regardless how I felt. I called the club, exited the freeway and reversed it back home. This info even gets sent to the CDC – Center for Disease Control, not my preferred database to be on.

With it having a contagion period, I was off work for three weeks, having to cancel or replace myself with another bartender on already booked gigs then. I pretty much stayed inside like a cave dweller. The next day I was down for the count. It hit me again, and this time, stayed. From that point, I had bi-weekly appointments with the doctor so he could keep measuring the levels of virus in the blood. I was in big trouble. It was high in my veins. The doctor was very afraid for me. My eyes and skin were becoming jaundice, and except for the gallons of water, I lost my appetite for food almost overnight. You get this type of thing from ingesting water or food that is contaminated with the virus. Hep A isn't from drugs or sex, that's more B and C.

Out of misery and desperation just after the contagious period was over, I sought out the help of an East Indian Herbalist in private practice, unknown to my doctor. I was essentially my own case of life and death at that point. I had nothing to lose. The Indian practitioner knew exactly what powdered herbs and capsules I needed, being all too familiar with the letters and degrees of Hepatitis. In the U.S., people suffer from A, B and C mainly, but where he's from and other countries, have different forms to deal with, I believe more deadly, like D, E, F, G, H, I and J, of which I was never previously aware of until now.

This stuff was nasty to have to get down my gullet on a daily basis or every other day. Sometimes I just couldn't do it, being too nauseous for me. But I did slowly recognize a change, where it seemed to somewhat cool the fire in the belly, a relief during any actual food intake through this marathon of barely alive. In those first few weeks, I lost muscle mass everywhere on my body – legs, arms and butt.

I became the master of disguise with eventually returning to work behind the bar, allowing for no more than 10 gigs a month, as I only had about 6 hours of good energy a day, plus it's recommended to do anything that requires movement or physical activity daily to keep everything else from shutting down. It would have been easy to sit around and do nothing, but I get bored really fast. My mind, therefore my body, has to do something.

I wore extra layers of clothing to not look bone rail thin with 25-30 lbs. loss of weight. I wore glasses and shades whenever I could get away with it. It was just to avoid people wondering, when everything at that stage was safe and okay. Arriving home at the end of gigs, I would at times park and sit in the truck for a couple minutes in silence, just to generate an ounce of power to get up the steps into the house.

All I was doing through this long, dark period was maintaining. I had nothing else, it was entirely stripped away. Dealing with this daily deprivation was maddening to say the least. You get so finished and enough already with it, and with the emotions that surface, I ended up in tears many times, barely holding on during the lowest power times.

I was ill with this devastating virus for 70 straight days before enough antibodies built up in my system to overtake it, kill it and kick it out. Believe me, you do not want this illness. There were times in that brutal period where it would have been just fine to die. The misery was that bad. What your tired mind goes through becomes a humbling, life-changing experience with survival. I went from the suffering and humiliation of dropping all those pounds with only 6 hours of good energy a day, to eating and drinking like a starving horse for two to three weeks with a ravenous hunger that hit, gaining my weight back after it left my body. If there's something good to come from this, it's the fact that you can never get it again. Your body's defense is now immune to it.

The virus was like being possessed by a demon from hell's gate. Here I was in great shape and I get rocked solid out of nowhere. The channel in which the biggest lessons in my life arrive are through medical illness or disease. It's been that way since childhood. I just hate it when it comes. But I always end up free and clear afterwards. I don't have any answers for it.

Below is the original piece I wrote seven years ago, while I was under attack from the virus, with more specific general detail, designed for any of the food and beverage magazines to consider running as a Health and Awareness story. They loved the article, but declined on publishing it, as it's not the most savory of subjects to go along with food and drink pairing. I agree. But it's out there, and you don't see it coming, nobody does. It's very elusive. That's the mystery of it, and why it's so important to be on the lookout. With the attempt of diligence in search of, I was never able to find out how I contracted the virus, because I work all over, not just in one establishment, making it almost impossible to pinpoint the who, what and where. Some months later, there was an outbreak of Hep A at a restaurant and bar in downtown L.A., where some 50 people became ill. It was all over the news, and kind of freaked me out again.

Awareness and Availability

Notification of vaccination for Hepatitis A

To __all__ food and beverage service personnel and management working in the Restaurant/Hospitality industry throughout the United States

With over 12 million people currently working in the industry, and an additional 270,000 entering the business each year (making it the largest employer outside the U.S. Government), it is of ever-increasing importance for all service personnel and management to become and to make aware of the availability of the Hepatitis A vaccine. It has been on the market for 10 years now, which is not a long time considering the number of people that should know about it, especially those of us who work in this business. Hepatitis A, in one sense, is like the worst form of food and/or water poisoning you could ever get. It is a liver illness caused by a virus entering/ingested in the body. You can get it by eating food (unclean or improperly cooked), drinking water that has the germ in it, or by close personal contact with a person who has it, but may or may not know that they have it. This is what makes it so dangerous, therefore potentially easy to innocently or accidentally pass it on to others, which can cause short strings of epidemics or outbreaks wherever they may arise or work.

The main problem is due to the early incubation/contagion period (average period is 28 days, but the range is 15-50 days) that may or may not come with symptoms. This beginning stage is crucial, because if the person does have symptoms come on, more than likely they won't know what they stem from or what they may be connected to, especially if they're not aware of what the symptoms of Hepatitis A are exactly, for a person with no symptoms can still give the illness to others. The person may not get early symptoms until the third week for example, or yet, may feel something of a very minor body sensation like a fever or being a bit tired for no reason, but would never think that it was soon to be connected to what could be a major illness. They may think its simple heat exhaustion, therefore may continue working without even knowing, but at some soon point in time the energy-clobbering symptoms will hit and they will hit hard. Along with the extreme energy loss, jaundice (yellowing of the skin and the white part of the eyes), dark urine, nausea, diarrhea, complete loss of appetite, stomach pain, and a thirst for liquids (major dehydration) at a level you've never felt before. You could drink a half-gallon of water and 10 minutes later you'd be parched. This is what makes it so important for everyone working in the F&B industry to know, is that it can hit anyone at anytime, even office personnel who eat or drink on-premise.

There is no treatment or medication for Hepatitis A once you get it and/or have been diagnosed by your doctor that you have it, through a blood test. It is a virus (viral illness) and antibiotics won't work. You basically have to allow it to run its course, which depending on the normal health of your body will take 45-90 days before you recover, and there are some individuals who can be ill for as long as 6 months. During this ill period you will also go through substantial weight loss (due to loss or reduction of appetite), will generally feel weak and will be thirsty all the time, so have plenty of fresh distilled water on hand to keep hydrated. Also, keep mobile with your body every day to a degree. Don't sit around all day and do nothing, even as drained as you may feel. Be a little active with a walk, a bike ride, some work. Your body is in survival mode.

After the initial contagious period is over after a couple few weeks, the only way to pass the disease on is through the stool. Casual contact does not spread the virus. Therefore, it is of utmost importance to keep your bathroom/toilet clean and disinfected/sanitized all the time, and utilizing the "Isolation Technique" is the best way to go. This means that anyone who has the illness should be the only one using a particular bathroom in the house, if at all possible. This helps insure the safety of everyone living in and around the same environment. Nobody wants to pass this devastating illness onto someone else. In fact, this illness is never the fault of the individual who gets it. It's always due to the negligence or not-knowing of the person who has it and decides to still go to work, and if that person is a food handler in a restaurant or bar, it couldn't get any worse of a risk than that. This is why management has the higher responsibility to make sure every person on staff is healthy with no colds or flu on the floor or behind the bar. Any staff employee should not be allowed to punch the clock.

Your diet will be trimmed down to what is the most easily digestible, so grains, rice, cereal, and pasta work best and also help to stabilize your weight while your appetite is low for just about anything. Your palate is turned upside down, so your favorite foods will make you nauseous to even think about. Above all, no dairy and no meat of any kind until your doctor notices some improvement. This means no milk in the cereal. For the benefit of your stomach, use a combination of aloe juice and pear or apple juice instead. Also, choose cereals that are low in sugar and higher in fiber and protein. Fruits are okay, but nothing too citric, as the key to eating during this period when the stomach bile is having a hard time not being able to work with the liver, is to avoid things that will cause/result in acid indigestion. Therefore, bananas, cantaloupe, or grapes may be a good starting point. You won't have a craving for much food for a period of time anyway, so keep it simple, bland, and easy to digest. The energy in your body has been heavily compromised and depleted, so don't tax it anymore than you have to, especially in the area of digestion.

There is only one good thing to come of this, and that is, once you've had it, you cannot get it again, as your body slowly develops antibodies (during illness) that kills the virus and kicks it out of your system, providing life-long protection, and you cannot transmit the virus to others. You also do not need to get a Hepatitis A vaccination shot. To prevent getting this nasty illness that wrecks you for a minimum of two months, check in with your doctor and inquire about the vaccine. The Hep A vaccine has an excellent safety profile, and it's only a one-shot stage, not a three-stage shot like Hep B is. The protection after receiving the Hep A vaccine begins four weeks after the dose has been administered. If you feel you've been exposed to the Hepatitis A virus, short-term protection is available by getting an immune globulin shot, which can be given before and within two weeks after coming in contact with someone who may have the virus.

Other ways to prevent are washing your hands before and after using the bathroom, and before eating. Wash all fruits and vegetables before eating them, drink bottled water, and eat only well-cooked foods when traveling.

To find out how and where children can get free shots, please call 1-800-427-8700. In looking at the world map of Hep A cases, the U.S. is low at somewhere between 50,000–100,000 cases a year, with the majority occurring more on the West coast than on the East coast, while countries like India and the province of Quebec are high, so be careful when you travel. Some of this information has been researched from text available on the L.A. County Health Dept. website: lapublichealth.org, the Center for Disease Control website: cdc.gov, and unfortunately from my own direct experience in late 2005.

MEDICAL UPDATE

As Gary Null reports from his weekly health show on Pacifica Radio dated Tuesday – January 24, 2006. He stated that intravenous Ozone Therapy, sessions of fresh oxygen into the blood-stream, kills the viral infection and knocks it out of the system. This therapy works for Hepatitis A, B, and C.

HEALING NOTE

An East Indian friend of mine informed me that the way to know if you've recovered from the illness is to eat candy. If it tastes sweet, then you're healthy. But if it tastes bitter, then you have not fully recovered. This is what I mean when I mentioned earlier of how this illness turns your palate upside down, making things you normally eat have a nasty taste on the palate.

14

ELEVATOR SKY MOVIE

I lay out my work clothes with method and a sense of order, somewhat like Jean Reno's character of Leon in the movie, The Professional, who with all his guns cleaned, loaded and cased, he sits in a chair in the dark, quieting his mind before he awakes and suits up for his next hired hit.

The bar gear sits in the passenger seat along with a selection of shirts; black, white, and a celadon green faded to perfection, to choose pending feel or required wear. That is, if they're not already hung in the back extra-cab of the truck from previous night's work. Always sporting inner shirts, I make my dress shirts go around a couple three gigs between dry cleans, hopefully avoiding the use of an iron for once-over, but at times a must. We all have our own ways of making things last.

The gig: A rooftop event on the 12th floor of a large condo building on Crescent Heights, a couple blocks down and south of Sunset Boulevard in Hollywood. That's one way to alleviate the fear of a 13th floor, by not even adding it. Honestly though, do we really think we avoid the 13th by calling it the 14th? I think not. It was the 40th birthday party for actress Salma Hayek's assistant. She threw it for herself and friends apparently, so it was not a surprise.

Driving through Joni Mitchell's favorite L.A. canyon, Laurel, its southern terminus is at Sunset Blvd., and becomes Crescent Heights Blvd. The bohemian spirit still endures there, as every year, residents gather for a group photograph at the country market. It was also immortalized by The Doors in their 1968 song "Love Street". The many legends of the canyon!

Parking is usually tight as a knot down there in the side streets surrounding the location of the event. The key is to get there at the right hour, wait if necessary, and pounce. There were only so many spots open under the building, and with a guest count of over 100 arriving later, people end up parking anywhere and everywhere. The earlier the better for me and the other bartenders, as we have a chance to just simply get there for a few minutes before we head in, to remove any potential driving stress en route, and for tying up any last moment communications with our cells.

I meet Chris and Kerry out on the street, and we walk in together. Taking the elevator to the top, it opens and we step around the corner to a door that leads out to the big, square roof where the party takes place. John and Pete's in LA delivered the booze and ice, and a party rental service supplied the bars and tables. The delivery guys had split up the beverage order and bags of cubes to both bars, a welcome relief from the norm.

Taking in the day before night overlook in all directions, breathing the air up there in for a few seconds, we quickly get to work on the full prep. We have an hour to rip through it. The caterer is a ways off in his own space, applying his own pace in the mobile galley set up for the passing of many apps, getting ready to grill the meats over the flame.

The DJ arrives, and she is really cute. She has a female co-captain with her, and a sideman to help with the heavy equipment. She was so hot, I didn't want her to lift a thing. With a dress that was slammin' short, it wasn't long before I started praying for a little wind beneath her wings. A sexy blonde with short hair! Who wasn't looking in her direction? But I kept it cool, with no interest in me being the one to create a thing. I was also working behind the bar with Heather, who I hadn't seen in a few years, so I was comfortable in catching up with her.

Dusk hit and dark soon after, cocktails, food and music were flowing with the many friends who came to celebrate. I remember it was a bit musty outside, a lukewarm temperature with some clouds in the sky, just the climate for thirst and hunger. It was a sizeable hangout, and who's not going to show up to a rooftop party with free juice, munchies and tunes? The visual was like a scene right out of a television episode, but all night long, with no "action", "cut" or "print".

It would be quiet a dozen floors up there, vertically away from the hustle on the streets, if it wasn't for the music filling the air with a certain energy that made one wonder if it was heard down below. There was no pool on the roof, but it was a sweet, silent getaway if you lived there, with plenty of open space to catch the sun on its downswing, or a place for a wet smoke and a good cry in a night rain. Add an umbrella, and you could be Gene Kelly. But if you're going to do that, you might as well fit the bill and throw on a nice suit.

The birthday girl appeared from her plush pad to start greeting her invitees, making the rounds with a measure of consistent effort. She was a very nice lady. Tina, the sexy DJ, made the first move over to my bar. Her petite close-up was sparkling, like I imagined it would, but I had no idea how she was going to make it through to the end with her next-to-bare wear without freezing to death with the eventual cool air shift.

Her order of two Tom Collins was an interesting surprise, given her youth. It made me feel as though she learned the classic drink watching her parents make them at home, or even more appropriately, her grandparents. Hard to know where to cut that generation break! Either way, it went well with her. We flirted at the bar for a couple minutes, and after she slowly walked back over to her spin platform, I was thinking after-party for two.

After our initial rush or two at the bar, Heather took over for a few minutes, and I disappeared to the far west side of the roof not being used, for a quick smoke and a drink, and a look over the safe railing down to the ground floor, high up with the Pacific Ocean invisible in the distant dark.

Slightly after the mid-point of the party, the on-screen beauty herself, Salma Hayek, shows up. I love it when a star like her braves it with a plain Jane look with little or no makeup. Not like she really needs any. But it shows you a different side to her – a bit known, a bit incognito, feeling safe around her assistant's friends.

I think to myself, as I'm writing this passage behind the bar at The Gardenia while the legendary Janis Paige is performing her show of songs and stories, "She's 89 years old." As I'm back and forth watching Janis and looking at this page of words, I realize that new Hollywood can never be old Hollywood, no matter who it is. Different work ethics, different media, a different dynamic shift altogether. It was simply a different time. Janis has been a Hollywood actress, singer and dancer since the 40's, and she still performs occasionally today. That's pretty amazing! Here's Janis below, dancing with Fred Astaire.

"I'm disappointed in acting as a craft. I want everything to go back to Orson Welles and fake noses and changing your voice. It's become so much about personality." Skeet Ulrich, actor

Chris, who's roaming around occupied with tray-passing, tells me he's been up and down from the roof party to her condo a half a dozen times. An indication that some small clique think they're more special than the rest of the party. The ones that don't want to be seen, yet aren't famous! I don't care much for inner circles. They're not that impressive when it comes down to brass tacks and longevity, more often fat than fiber. People with real talent don't have to play that. However, the Hollywood machine is very competitive to make it in and be successful. It's not only what and who you know, but living out a tough existence of few wins and many losses. Ultimately, my hat is off for the many who take the time to persevere and navigate through the unforgiving maze.

As another example, at this passage I'm now at my writing sanctuary near home, Michael D's Café, at the counter, and sitting two chairs over is the actor, Joe Don Baker, who became famous in the 70's when he portrayed Tennessee sheriff Buford Pusser in Walking Tall, but has been acting since the mid-60's. It was 6:30 pm and we were both having breakfast and chatting a little bit. He was in Junior Bonner with Steve McQueen, as well as Cape Fear, The Killing Time, and three 007 films, just to name a few of the 80 credits he has in his career. Joe Don has a new movie coming out next year called Mud, with Matthew McConaughey, Reese Whitherspoon, and Sam Shepard. He's 76 now, has been in the business for six decades, and he doesn't make a big issue of himself. He's totally cool to hang and talk with. After reading the paper for a while, he gets a piece of apple pie to go, and drives off in either his old 240Z or his Citroen SM. Very cool!

Joe Don Baker - on working with Sam Peckinpah in Junior Bonner (1972) "I didn't care for Peckinpah at all. He was one of those little guys who tries to bully big guys and he almost got his ass whipped for trying to do it to me. Every time I was going to throttle Peckinpah, Steve McQueen would come over and calm me down like a brother would"

Many parties are filled with starving artists and misfits of all types trying to make it, getting some exposure and name recognition. Some stick around for the long haul, and others go back home to where they came from. It's a natural revolving door occurrence in this town of lost souls. You get used to it with no matter or bother about it, especially after you've worked well over a thousand one-off events with a bar. I smile and pour, instantly becoming part of the overall gathering.

After 11:00 pm or so, we slowly start fading out and boxing up excess products we're not going to use behind the bar. There are always leftovers, but we were lucky to go through quite a bit, resulting in less schlepping at the end. It's the one drag difference between this work and working in an actual bar. But I do both so, I just deal with it, as it's always something no matter where you work or what you do.

It may rain, so we get the bars broken down and inside the top floor hallway, with the product going in a small storage/utility room nearby. We take all the open bottles to the birthday girl's condo for a quick drop-off a few floors down. Back up for a final clean-over outside, I head over to the elevator with my pack of tools over shoulder. It opens, and there's Tina the DJ, making out with the sound tech assistant. Thinking to myself "Wait a second, I thought you'd be saving that for me?" I immediately tell him that he'd better grab his sound board and speakers that were against the wall in the hallway before they get stolen.

Surprisingly, the poor lug did what I told him, as it was a chance move to get her alone. Nothing could ever become serious with it, just some playtime. I punched the button to the ground floor, but she held it open for him instead of letting us ride alone. Away gathering his blocks of equipment, I came up behind her and put my fingers under her G-string to convince her otherwise, as I knew they were going back down to the party inside. No dice! The deal had already been struck. A closer convenience won out. Those precious lust-filled moments dissipate into thin air as the three of us take the elevator together, not to be seen again. L.A. is like a universe, where you never run into the same night stranger.

I get to my truck, put my tan fleece coat on, and light a smoke standing on the sidewalk. It's going to come down from the sky. Just a matter of time, I can smell it in the air. We avoid a drench with no cover . . .

15

A Stop Along The Trail

In 2010, I get a call from a private catering outfit for an area of aristocratic society in L.A., to bartend a small political fundraiser over in the Wilshire corridor for a lady who was reported to be quite connected in this arena of questionable motivations with our nation's leaders. Soon enough, the reason became clear. The guest attendees and speakers for the evening were none other than Barbara Boxer, Al Franken, and John Kerry.

The high rises in Westwood certainly don't rent or sell to the poor. You have to be loaded to get into one of these plush floors of luxury, and it doesn't hurt that you have no interest or wanting anything to do with yard work or mowing lawns. However, with ownership of one of these properties, it leaves no doubt more time available to do what you like and prefer giving time to, the ultimate freedom of choice. We all strive for expanded levels of that in our lives. It's interesting to hang out with people who have more of it than most, even for just a little while.

This wasn't my first time in for an event or party to see this lifestyle with my own eyes, so I was used to the standard entrance procedure of "Sign in Stranger". But this time we all met in the underground parking in the rear of the building and took the service elevator to the 20th Floor. Sort of like being there and not being there! No problem, I love being invisible and making money. I wish I could do it more, like the ability to emanate a duplicate physical presence of myself and work two places at the same time. Kyle Branche – The Bi-locating Bartender!

I can dream . . .

The crew of us walked in. Security met us at the door, paid for by the people. The staff had been there before, but it was my first gig at this residence. I just followed and listened initially, until I found my workspace to start setting up. It was one of those extremely rare occurrences where I had to tend bar out of one of those tall, wide cabinet-against-the-wall bars. The kind that opens up, wishing you could hide inside instead of attempting to operate like a professional while my backside was in open view and proximity to anyone walking by. Not the normal positioning bartenders are used to. Thankfully, it was off to the side, so most only saw one ass cheek hidden by all black attire and apron.

Swallowing what little pride I had left for humility to take the wheel, I just said fuck it and started getting things done. It was all very nice, expensive ware to work with, along with my kit, but the physical position was a bother at the beginning. I had everything I needed for the night, though. That usually gets me through the motions I've performed thousands of times before in various settings all over town, whether in a real bar establishment, makeshift or from scratch.

Had I known in advance, I would have slipped a mind-alterer down my throat to replace my artificial grin with a real smile. It was only for a few hours though, so I just dug my heels in more wanting to see a close-up of what goes on at this money-grabber over appetizers, cocktails and speaking. After decades in the field, I simply surrender and make it work for me. The pay is all virtually the same, in fact, with private gigs like this it's guaranteed, which is even better.

No more mysteries of working full-time in one venue wondering if it's going to be busy or not, and jockeying for the best shifts. With a shitty economy like we have today, it's even more difficult to rely on a sole source to cover the bills, especially in the world of bar work where the last thing that prevails is security and stability. You can have good runs with hot clubs, of which I have had many times over the years, but there's always a time where you end up moving on, for a variety of reasons.

I was introduced to the host/client, a well-to-do woman in her late 70's. She was very nice and displayed all the proper etiquette you might expect. This is what usually dictates my game of mannerisms to match. Wherever I work, it's always best to blend in precisely to the given environment and crowd. A temporary shape-shifting of one's personality and movement to what's going on around, providing a warm fitting with whatever collective energies swirling in the air.

She was a staunch Democrat. And even though there's nothing wrong with having a strong constitution in any interest or concern that's safe and doesn't cause harm to others, the sense that most of us get when we think of politics at this level is that it's anything but. I've been around died-in-the-wool Republicans for 10 hours straight at the Reagan National Library (an earlier story I wrote on my blog, titled "Secret Serviced"), so I'm familiar enough with how people of influence ride.

With the thought of both the big political parties of this country in mind, you get a sneak peek into the eventual realization that many of their actions are not all that different from each other. Not when the color of money is the same, and spends the same way too. It's just the strange feeling of this underlying aggression on the trail of a campaign year (I hate calling it a season) that seems to run through their veins a little hotter when preoccupied in getting what they want, letting nothing get in the way of their stately post, income stream, or having any part of it being taken away. Another game of sport, with winners and losers, and little left over for the majority.

The worst addiction there is to humankind. The tribe of "Never Enough" seems to never end! Why is there no drug to settle these financial maniacs down, just a hair or two? Regardless, I have the best seat in the house, the bench, the bleachers, the bar, whatever you want to call it. I get to pour, mix, shake, stir and roam. The position of no permanent attention from anyone – my favorite hideout in the open!

The invitees started arriving, some 40 guests in total. Not big in count, but considering it was all confined to an interior, it soon got a bit tight and claustrophobic, with the only exit for fresh air a balcony for three or four. The atmosphere soon became loud with chatting and mingling as I was handling the initial rush of drink with a good peripheral vision of oncoming to my left. Barbara Boxer and Al Franken arrived either together or close to the same time towards the first third of the reception, while John Kerry came through the door shortly after most of the guests had been accounted for. As for celebs, the legendary songwriting couple of Alan and Marilyn Bergman attended the gathering as well.

People had to start spreading out from the hovering in the living room in order for appetizers to get passed through, for a spill of any kind was to be avoided at all costs. Due to the literal white carpet treatment, there was also no red wine or cranberry juice being poured. Fine with me, as it completely alleviated any accidental drippage from my higher end of potential risk, the turn of the pour.

Surrounding the huge, centered coffee table and window space floor-to-ceiling for a good look at the city, the once-combustible energies of the group early on slowly shifted to one of relax, calm and maintain. It was needed, as at some point a degree of quiet would have to overcome the room for the White House elite to commence with their words.

The host spoke over the crowd trying to warmly get everyone's attention, and after saying a few things to begin, she was interrupted by Ms. Boxer with not the most pleasant of hand-offs, and Barbara took over. Nobody said anything, but it was kind of odd to stand there and witness a moment of impatient aggression like that, as though in a hurry to get the ball rolling to avoid being late for the private jet that takes them to Sacramento. So she starts in with the Democratic mission, their accomplishments to date and what they're trying to achieve in their respective positions in the future, while holding on to what they got.

I can't imagine how difficult it must be on Capitol Hill to be constantly splitting logs to get good bills passed for the people. How many good bills have failed, and how many bad bills have passed? You have to ask what drives them to continue working steadfast for decades in a quicksand nightmare. People that are actually into politics as some form of personal gain are a strange breed, almost non-human, though they always want you to think and believe otherwise. Serving your country in these capacities is a great thing, but turning yourself into a career politician is another, and the hard-working citizens of our land know all too well what that spells.

Following Barbara into the speaking fold was Al Franken. Most of us in the room in their 40's and 50's mainly remember him from SNL, so one can't help but to look and listen to him in an expected somewhat comedic mode. He didn't disappoint. Though he took less time at the stand, he probably had everyone's attention more than the others, therefore getting his content on average to seep in deeper. Earlier in the evening I had taken a quick walk through the crowd when I had about a minute to do so, though I didn't care much for leaving my post in this specific situation. I basically ended up right next to him at one point trying to slip through and around. I don't know how much makeup he uses for the camera, but he had to be one of the whitest white guys I've ever seen, a pale look in sort of a healthy way.

The waiters would go back and forth from the kitchen to the main room, so I was the only staffer out there the entire time. I was a fly on my own wall! How could I not absorb the surroundings, the position requires it, like I do working anywhere else. I have to be on top of it at some functions more than others. It's the changing nature of each individual event as it takes place.

John Kerry held up the rear with a convincing speech of progress for the country and the economy, but it also circled around the ideals of the Democratic Party and what they would like for positive change. It was all good stuff for the most part, but to people like me in the room, the words and actions have to come together as one, or else the words are just a temporary air space where the foundation doesn't follow.

The one thought that stayed with me most was when Ms. Boxer worded a paragraph of her dish in regards to monies that made me feel as though the wealthy upper class are simply in cahoots with keeping the status quo. The one area they don't want jeopardized, holding onto it like a mean guard dog. At the end, guests got out their checkbooks and away they went.

This occasion was very similar to one I worked in 2008, a Jewish fundraiser at a private home in Beverly Hills with close to 100 attending, that included Hillary Clinton speaking with L.A. Mayor Antonio Villaraigosa opening up for her. This huge home with hardwood floors became a red wine symphony for the guests, and the very nice built-in bar where I took stage was right in the middle of it all.

Most who attend are rich, political donators to the cause, their cause, primarily voting to keep more for themselves, not what's good for all. The rich have more to gain and/or lose than the rest of us, which is why they participate more. Campaigning and voting is just a long, expensive show to give the majority the illusion that we matter to them. We don't! There are no candidates of real presidential stature anymore. It's all out in the open. No longer can anything be concealed for what it really is.

The pressure was relieved as guests started leaving in quick fashion. I cleaned up the bar and closed the cabinet, finishing just as the rest of the staff were completed in the kitchen. It was time to catch the service elevator back down to parking so we could all share in the reloading of the van before we headed back up and out to our own vehicles. I just had a smaller pack for a bar kit over my shoulder in place of the normal size for this occasion, always a nice relief to walk in with less.

It was getting cold outside that close to the ocean. I slid on my coat in a still-wired moment, as it usually takes a little time to get my head back to normal and settle down from those high levels of attention and awareness to the service of others. Turning on the radio to my favorite Jazz station out of Long Beach, enjoying the time where I catch perfect reception on that side of the hill, I light a smoke and sit back in recline, wanting to disappear to another world more fair and sane, instead of existing in this ultimate theatre of economic pain and financial fuck-over for an entire country that didn't deserve it . . .

16

PARTY OF 8

Pulling up into what was once known as The Jewel of Los Feliz, an area up in the hills just off of Van Ness Avenue and Hollywood Freeway, I realize how close it is to many historical points down below on flatter ground. Just a couple minutes away is Beachwood Drive, the original sight of the old Hollywoodland neighborhood, where Aldous and Laura Huxley once lived in the late 50's, early 60's, on Deronda Drive. Scenes from the 1956 classic film "Invasion of the Body Snatchers" were shot in front of the Beachwood Market and Village, as well as a scene in David Lynch's "Mulholland Drive" of a scary guy in a cowboy hat in a deserted corral at the top of Beachwood Canyon, which is the same area where the Sunset Ranch is located today, a large horse stable for the public to take toured night rides through the Hollywood Hills.

I've worked several gigs on Beachwood over the last decade, but a couple years ago there was a gig I couldn't work – the season-ending wrap party for the producers and cast of the show "In Treatment" with Gabriel Byrne. That was a drag, as he's one of my favorite actors to watch.

Just South at Beachwood's beginning is Franklin Avenue, home of the castle-like Church of Scientology Celebrity Centre International building a block down that before it was purchased by L. Ron Hubbard in 1973, was the landmark Chateau Elysees. The church is now known for owning more historical buildings in Hollywood than any other entity, some $400 million worth. I remember going over there and checking it out over 20 years ago when I was in a bit of a lost and search mode myself. It wasn't bad. It was different, that's for sure. I talked with some people there, but never signed up to become a paying member or regular participant. That's when it became kind of questionable for me, so I backed off for a bit and never returned. I didn't have the excess funds to start paying them some regular monthly dues. Nothing wrong with it, we all make choices, some benefit, some regret. But hey, at least we're seeking ways to improve and do something instead of just grazing the earth all the time. Then again, maybe that's what we should be doing!

I finally wrap a right turn onto Live Oak, the point of my destination. I spend a few minutes of early time gazing over the hazy city and downtown before the remaining light turns into night. I was told that across the street is the home of actress, Kelly Lynch. Chris, my waiter friend, pulls up, who knows where everybody lives, as I mentioned before, his brother owns the security company that some celebs and the wealthy use on property. The last time him and I were here, at the end of the night I followed him back down a different path than I usually take up. I know a lot of streets, but Chris makes me feel like I just arrived in L.A. You know how it goes, right when you think you know everything about anything, someone comes along and changes your game!

Chris tells me to watch out for his left arm signal, as my headlights tight-tail his new sports car down the narrow, windy pitch-black road, where it's all too easy to slam into a street can sticking out too far for the following morning's trash pick-up. That's one thing you notice, especially in the alleys of Beverly Hills, their dump cans are so fucking big you could fit six people in them. They have twice as many in total than any middle-class neighborhood. But that's how it goes - the more you own, the more you shit-can. In many ways, I'm glad I'm not rich, but there are times where I could use it on occasion, just for continued encouragement in the one life that I have.

I catch Chris's hand movement, he slows down and I do the same. He points across his vehicle to let me know of the main entry gate into the huge Brad Pitt/Angelina Jolie compound, which from what I gathered is like four surrounding properties in one, bought up over the last several years, creating a sort of magic kingdom, so close but just far away enough, hidden and unmarked. And it's only 8-10 properties down from where we're working tonight.

Chris parks a few spaces in back of my truck. If both of us had passengers, they would open the door and slice into either a streamline of well-groomed shrubbery or a mail box would be spinning off its hinges. With no sidewalks, the landscaping takes advantage all the way up to the asphalt. Jody, the other server for the night, is sitting in her car, and we all walk in together, as the main gate was still closed. Better to open once!

Hillary and Adam are great clients and have been for years. They're super cool people, and their single-level ultra-tech modern home is actually combined with substantial land and yard, compared to other edge properties within walking distance, that are all house and no grass. No mower, just hedge clippers necessary, for the gardener that is!

The main house help answers the door, and we stroll in. In the attempt to assume our positions, I was at a loss for mine. I couldn't find the bar, which was usually a large portable on the outside patio. Thinking it was going to be another of the same type of party and normal guest count of 40-50, it soon became clear that I didn't receive the same memo. Thinking to myself for a moment "What the hell am I doing here, I could have worked another gig elsewhere tonight". Hillary appears in the living room area and let's me know it's a small dinner party, not with the usual crowd of friends. They have a small built-in bar, but more of the cottage/bungalow style, of which the home deserved better. The only thing missing that would make the house complete, a custom build-out and step-behind.

I go to the kitchen and find out that Chris and Jody had the more clear and accurate event details, which still made me wonder what I was doing there. Limbo and I don't get along very well, either I'm in gear with task and purpose, or I prefer to be in neutral, but on my own time, not someone else's. Eventually I realize I have to somehow fit into the mold of the evening's activities or just put on a coat and become the house butler, nodding and walking away!

Adam was in the kitchen executing the role of chef with precision, and Hillary held her own in the dessert department. Lurking on the countertop was a 1.5 Liter bottle of a 1970 Chateau Paullac, unopened. What to do? I create a makeshift bar set-up in the kitchen to double as a station and hiding place, assembling whatever I could think of in close proximity with everything else. They soon realized that putting a task-mastered workhorse like myself in this quasi-helper position was the wrong thing to do. They thought that I knew, but I was previously unaware. I just needed more reason to sustain me and I'm fine, easy to work with. But asking to give me something to do after 30 years of shredding at top game was almost an embarrassment, if not an accidental touch of humiliation.

I'm a professional in this business, not some wannabe actor biding time for a guest-starring spot. There was no bad intention by anyone, but how do I remove that from my face to feel more at home and useful than just the role of a floater. However, I do have to keep in mind that they put me on this gig because of who was coming. The daunting news of the guests included Barbra Streisand, James Brolin, Mia Sara, Brian Henson (son of Jim Henson), along with the head of Universal/Sony and his wife. Surprise!

Adam goes about the cork removal at a brisk pace, not considering the decades it had been stuck in glass. We were about to find out the mystery if a 40-year wine was too long in the bottle or not. The older and/or mislayed the bottle of wine is, the more patient and sensitive you have to be with the cork. There are also slightly different cork lengths that one cannot always see. Removing the top foil helps, but the bottle could be too dark anyway. After the client had initially used his corkscrew without being successful, I was able to remove the rest of it, the last third of the cork remaining, intact at the very bottom, so no loose ends fell into the wine.

He was impressed! I was shocked!! I didn't think it was going to come up. Either way, we could have used a simple cheesecloth to filter anything out, but there wasn't a need after I cleaned the inside of the bottle neck of any minute debris. It's just better if it's a clean removal all in one pull. Some corks are tougher, so you need to take your time with a very slow screw upward and work it. With love and care, there was no dust in the drink. Not an easy thing to do. We decanted it for close to 3 hours before the guests first tasting at the sit-down, giving it substantial breathing time. I cleaned the bottle up really nice afterward and put it on the back counter. Luckily, there was very little residual in the bottom remains.

Cocktails and hors d'oeuvres begin the beguine. Glancing out of my kitchen peephole with curious eyes, out of all the places in the world a legend could be right now, she was right here. Barbra Streisand. The one and only. And since I used to watch Marcus Welby M.D. as a kid, I was equally familiar with James Brolin. He's a big dude. Intimidation usually has to do with personality, ego, voice and energy. If they're warm, you feel it, if they're otherwise, you feel that too, all caught in a matter of seconds. This dictates and therefore arcs how Chris, Jody and I will be conducting and behaving with our collective mannerisms and floor choreography. The initial greeting and reception lasted a little less than an hour.

Steady as she goes . . .

When it came to the food, I let Chris and Jody tell me what to do and where to go. Though at the beginning after the guests took their named places at the long dining table is where I timely made first entrance with the decanter of the precious 1970 red, praying it was of good taste, even with Adam giving it a swish on the palate earlier, not everyone has the same tongue of acceptance. It was fine, but reaching, pouring and breathing in times eight while moving around the table, well, of course I had to be the first one, with the least experience. This just can't not happen, now can it? Will the heavens ever stop testing me? I make it around the curve with silent lucidity, and slip away into the kitchen taking air deep into lungs, cooling the beginnings of perspiration on my forehead.

Chris and Jody followed to the table with rolls and butter. My breather was short. Next was a thin, cream-based soup, much easier to spill than a salad. Oh, the challenges never end! Hillary and Barbra were sitting next to each other on the corner of the L closest to the kitchen entrance. Of course that's where I was told to go. It was closer, but I don't know about any easier! With Hillary to my right and Barbra to my left, I slowly plated in front and over their beautiful hands, one at a time. With the final lean left, Barbra abruptly got up and brushed her body across my outstretched arm and went to the ladies room. Looking at where Chris and Jody were at with their drops, I did an about face and rolled out of the area to grasp one more bowl to reverse back my way to Mia Sara. Soup was done.

Adam cooked Kobe beef and lobster in sealed bags in boiling water to hold all the juices in. There was a vegetable and au gratin potato to complete the dish. The plating and removing at the tables continued, as well as my double-duty with wines and waters while trying to feel the right balance of being there and not being there, avoiding any intrusion to multiple conversations that were not to our privy. We had enough to do and sweat over, as the kitchen wasn't exactly cool in temperature. I always thought Streisand was gorgeous, and the close-up was no disappointment.

All went well, but working with extremely tall, sensitive stemware for the champagne and wines white and red is a freaky issue, not to mention the decanter itself, as you're trying to avoid any breakage or shattering at all costs. Then you have to do your best at proper pouring and multiple dish/course placement at the large table, moving in-between guests, without fumble! In fact, there was more focus on those safety measures than being tripped out by the celebs attending. This is how a dinner party goes! I perform this type of service too infrequently to be really good at it. By the time it comes around again, I've forgotten what I had previously learned, as far as left and right, etc. I'm not at my best when I'm out from the bar, but I always give it a go for sake of new experience. And the clients had faith in us to help them pull the evening off without a hitch.

I always thought Streisand was gorgeous, and the close-up was no disappointment. She had a casual and simply beautiful look about her that evening, little make-up because she doesn't need any, really. And she seems smaller and cuter in person than what the camera does to her. I hadn't seen Mia Sara in a long time, maybe since *Ferris Bueller's Day Off* or *Timecop,* but she's done more TV, episodic and voiceover than film since those days, still in it. And then you have the head of Universal/Sony Pictures, that pretty much has more power than anyone at the table, with Adam his VP. That's the connection for this dinner taking place.

With dessert as the closer, Hillary took control of the kitchen with Adam keeping at the table this time. I think we had three different selections on each plate for the guests who had more than one sweet tooth flavor craving. It was quite the incredible culinary atmosphere despite having no hired chef on premise covering all the bases. It was more of a shared in-house event only to avoid some ugly, beat-up catering van outside in the driveway. Clean and safe, no green bean deliveries in a large, aluminum tin!

Jody was doing most of the washing in the sink with both Chris and I helping a little when we could. There's a point where the table needs three servers, than two servers, and finally one server towards the end, as a kind of fade-in and fade-out experience, much like the movies. We were the acts that created our own silent film that night, that's always the attempt anyway, moving around in whispering code talk like a more calm, attractive version of the three stooges in dinner service attire, looking at each other in passing, keeping busy for time to move quicker.

Nothing dropped, nothing spilled, nothing broken, nothing slipped. Like a dance on eggshells, we made it through the night. If a Chef or Head Waiter would have been there, they would've caused the potential friction for everything to fall apart at every nail. That's what they do, getting paid to provide the pins and needles that we don't need.

After the star-studded cast left, there were the five of us.

17

QUIET ON THE SET

Occasionally, I get the call to work bar gigs at the various movie studios here in L.A., whether it be Culver City, Studio City or Universal City. There are others, like Warner Brothers/Burbank studios, but some have their own sort of built-in culinary catered event department on the lot when they occur somewhat consistent, using an on-call staff in-house. They rarely go outside the walls unless it's either a large event or one with very short notice.

Universal is like that to a degree, but once in a while I get to sneak in if the show's offices has their own budget and petty cash. It all depends on the timing of everything, last minute or plenty of notice with advance booking. The studio lots are like very busy production villages all to themselves. They don't let you in the gates unless they know exactly what you're doing there. And parking can often be a ways away. I may be able to drop my bar gear off at the stage door, but I may end up walking a distance back.

When I have a call time to arrive, it's always good to get on site up to a half-hour early to allow for the unexpected that can suck up minutes, just in case. Through the gates I get my pass, stage number and directions. Sometimes I can set up early, and if they've requested me to bring my own custom bar set-up, that means extra dragging time with a few more trips back and forth. I may have to wait for prep if the bar is close to the set and they're already taping with a live audience. The many variables that you don't know until you arrive.

The beverage product could be right there close by or it could be at a major schlepping distance. However, the studios usually have plenty of help hanging around wanting something to do, and these days I have no problem accepting help from others, especially those who make good money with the union along with health insurance and other perks and bennies that I don't have.

You notice with unions that employees have a tendency to work together as a team, covering and having each other's backs, unlike the private sector where it's more shark infested. I like their upside a lot better than I do my downside! The idea and feeling of being taken care of is very motivating to me, makes me want to do more, not less. But the Food and Beverage industry is not of the same mindset to take care of their own.

Given its size of overall work force throughout the country, you'd think it would be of automatic necessity. It's just the opposite. Hospitality as a whole prefers not to have strong, dedicated people they can rely on for long term. Let's put it this way – they talk it, but they don't walk it, and they certainly don't back it. It must have something to do with seeing these various positions as menial tasks of work regarded as servile, when in reality they are very much respected professions. Just ask Europe.

Now if I can just figure out where the ice bags are?

One of the first gigs I got on the set was a final season episode wrap party for the TV comedy series "Less Than Perfect", starring Eric Roberts, Andy Dick, and Sara Rue over at CBS Studio Center on Radford Ave. in Studio City. I remember being right off the soundstage and having to set up very quietly while it was all happening live. After each take I could move more freely, but as soon as I heard the words "Quiet on the Set", I become the silent mover in the shadows. I bring my rubber hex floor mats for the back bar so, if something drops, it won't break and will barely register a sound that reverberates any distance at all. I may bring a lot of tools with me, but it's for good cause. The production assistants appreciate it.

Following the last scene of the script, you hear the words "It's a Wrap". The pressure of the set is relieved, and it's party time. A few chosen winners are plucked out of the audience to join in the festivities and mingle with the stars, the DJ starts up the music, the food catering floor staff begins passing appetizers, and I start making drinks at rapid pace, handling it all solo behind the bar. It's always hectic at first until you catch up to the wave, and then you just ride it into shore.

This position I have and maintain is pretty much front and center with everyone attending; producers, directors, actors, cameramen, grips, assistants, office personnel, audience members, you name it. I have to be on my best energetic game. There is no option with only one of me behind the bar that all are counting on to pull it off. The eyes are on me once again, but I can focus and execute with the best of them. When you have enough experience doing one thing for so long, you can dial it in pretty tight, making the performance right on the mark.

It was great to meet Eric Roberts when he came to the bar. He was very nice, cordial and even asked how I was doing. People must see the comfortable couch and smile in my eyes when I'm working, easy to approach and chat up. I love it when the bar becomes the hanging-out point for many.

Years ago I got called to be one of several bartenders for the Producers Guild Awards that were held on the lot of the Culver Studios in Culver City, which is just northeast of MGM Studios. It was literally held in the huge stage where many movie classics were shot, including "Citizen Kane", "Gone With The Wind", the original "King Kong" with Fay Wray, "E.T.," and Hitchcock's

"Notorious". But this was only one of 13 soundstages on the property. So many more movies and even TV shows were shot here, including "Hogan's Heroes", "Batman", "Gomer Pyle", "The Twilight Zone" with Rod Serling, "Lassie", "The Andy Griffith Show", and the pilot episodes of the original "Star Trek".

We get there very early to unload and set-up, everyone lending a helping hand with the beverages for a guest count of hundreds. This was one of those size parties where *the more the merrier* doesn't quite apply on our end. There can be an overload of initial product in to cover,

and depending on what doesn't get used up, could be equally taxing when it's the end of the night. We usually pray we're so busy that there's nothing left for us to re-box and load back. I remember it was chilly and rainy out that evening, as this event takes place at the beginning of the year when it's still officially winter in Southern Cal. The bones can get a little brittle in knowing that our body adjustment to cold weather here is the same as someone else's skin being adapted to living in Minnesota, except thirty more degrees closer to zero!

They were serving full plated dinner at the tables, so there's a point where the bar slows down in the middle of the evening, and we take turns with breaks for a few to avoid sleeping standing up like horses. Gigs can be busy all the way through or it can have a series of ups and downs, you only know about half the time going in. It would be great if all the bars would be in the main room surrounding the tables, it might help us keep busier with the guests knowing there in quicker walking range, but they would also be in the peripheral camera eye, so the floor waiters have to put on the extra mileage to keep the show looking clean and wholesome.

Last year I worked the actual set bar for a live audience table reading with the cast of "Hot in Cleveland" back at CBS in Studio City, I think it was Stage 19. There were three of us bartenders for this gig, so Andrea and Daniel worked alongside me at this medium-length bar with a walk space in between. With almost 200 guests invited, the studio can easily afford a slight overstaff when they deem necessary, making my job a little easier sharing the duties.

A Cabaret friend, actress and performer at The Gardenia club, Robyn Spangler, was part of the reading, and showed up with her husband to say hello before she had to hit the stage. This also takes me back to when I used to see Valerie Bertinelli at Lakeside Golf Club, and now she's back in the game, on this show. It's interesting to work a sort of shell bar on the set where the front and top is the real deal, but the back under bar is not of normal use, you get to see a lot of props and leftover knick-knacks gathering dust until their next use on-camera.

A couple months after, I was called back there on another soundstage, in a makeshift living room/lounge area for the executives, with no ceiling, as just on the other side of the thin wall they were taping the pilot episode of a new comedy show called "Only Fools and Horses", that starred Christopher Lloyd, John Leguizamo, and Wendi McClendon-Covey from "Reno 911". This shoot was a basic pass or fail, with the onlooker suits watching a live tape feed linked into a large TV monitor/screen in the room where I was cornered to pour.

In fact, the director of the show was actor and ex-L.A. Ram defensive end, Fred Dryer, His voice saying "Action" and "Cut" several times over was easily recognizable. This 30-minute pilot took nearly 4 hours to complete shooting. It was a pretty funny show, but with this includes all the re-takes, forgetting or screwing up lines of dialogue, and hearing Leguizamo cussing at himself. To think the bank these performers make, yet the script and marks still have to be memorized and hit, and the money doesn't improve the memory. And on top of that, you still have to act. It made for a long, drawn out night for me, especially with only mild activity at the bar. One executive came over to me a few times with rolling eyes that told me "Get this over with so I can go home". The show was cool, but I don't think it received the green light for a season's worth.

Late last year and early this year, I got the call on two different occasions, during weeknights (Tues, Wed, etc) which is perfect, of which the other studio gigs were the same so it doesn't clash with my weekend work, to bring my custom bar and set-up inside the production offices of the show "Guys with Kids" up at Universal City for episode and season wrap parties, with the hope they'll get picked up for another season. It was great to meet the crew; Anthony Anderson, Jesse Bradford, Tempest Bledsoe, along with the creators and writers, and saying hello to Jamie-Lynn Sigler put a nice lift in my step. She's just as gorgeous in person.

Their offices are like a creative playground, with three massive bean bags and other toys. I set the bar up right on the outside of the office where the long table sits the various show writers and all the 3x5 cards stuck to a wall board taking you scene-by-scene through the episode. I love to see and learn the process of all the inner workings of the entertainment business. There's no doubt had I grown up in L.A., I would have been in the business in some capacity, either in back or in front of the camera. However, with my look and baby face, I should probably feel grateful not getting eaten up and thrown out as a child actor. Instead, I'm the pleasant observer putting cocktails in hand.

Back in 2007, also up at Universal, I worked both in the production offices and up on the roof for parties for then President of NBC-Universal Television, Katherine Pope. She was very nice, and I ended up working a couple gatherings at her home as well. She's now the executive producer of the TV series "Touch" with Kiefer Sutherland. Now that I think about it, I've also worked a couple private party gigs at the home of Amanda Segel, who is now the supervising producer of the show "Person of Interest", but back when I saw her last I think she was co-producing the last two seasons of "Without a Trace". Shows come and go to the activity and rating numbers of the viewers.

It's funny, as I write this story, I get a call today from a service I work out of to possibly pull a 10-12 hour bar gig at old Paramount Studios over on Melrose, for a whiskey brand that's doing some sort of sponsored event expecting close to 250 people throughout the day and eve. That's a long-ass haul, as I may have to bring my own bar again along with other details and particulars to solo manage. This call also reminded me that I worked a gig there almost 10 years ago that I forgot, and then jogged my memory even further that I once worked at Raleigh Studios as well. That's as far back as I can remember, which now means the only major studio I haven't worked a bar gig at is Warner Brothers in Burbank. But now that I think deeper, something tells me I did a day thing there. Hmmm, oh well . . . end of mind.

Rolling . . . Speed . . . Marker . . . Set . . . Action!

18

A GLASS OF CABARET

Only a tiny percentage of establishments in the food and beverage entertainment business survive the test of time. Most go for a few years and disappear for a variety of both legitimate and suspect reasons that individuals like myself, are all too familiar with seeing in the world of hospitality and nightlife. They can be here one day and gone the next.

The Gardenia Room has been my occupational hub away from home off and on, in and out, for close to 24 years now, a length of tenure unexpected of me. With working the bar at the club, it's allowed me the flexibility to also work with many other establishments and outfits, practicing and expanding what I do, which included a 9-year stint writing for the industry magazines.

But I guess I've grown and come to some sense of maturity over 30 years where I've learned to accept more than contend and repair. A relief for me of sorts, when your mind is a creative castle of ideas and production, it became a necessary outlet. A metabolism built for speed finally paces itself into cruise control for the long run.

Of course, that was the main reason and /or problem for any early arguments that Tom and I had back when we were younger, of which were mostly my fault. I was young and still growing. Well, that and just a few unnecessary dramas. It's the restaurant business, scuffles and mistakes exist. Tom and Bruce, the owners of the club have always kept the door open for me, even at times when I didn't know it. We've seen each other go from our late 20's and 40's to our early 50's and 70's, employers and their employee.

At times, Tom will come and sit at the bar, just after the doors open when the bar is set-up and the room/floor is ready for another night, as he hands me the bank to count into our "old school ching-ching" National cash register, with the caught glimpse silently saying to each other "We're still here". After all these years, we could run the place sleepwalking, a surreal quality haunting the hallowed ground created 33 years ago. The same goes for Nichole and Leonel who've also been on the clock for a combined quarter century or more, those numbers also qualify. It's a small room, the less come and go, the better.

The Gardenia is the longest-running Cabaret Supper Club in the United States. It deserves some recognition for its staying power. The credit goes to Tom and Bruce. They could have cashed out long ago and made life easier on themselves, but sometimes it's better just to have something to do than to exist with too much open every day time, unless you have a huge garden to tend to at home. I think it was the right move, for purposes of dual longevity, and keeping a rare art form alive, though it's gained in popularity somewhat over the last decade especially.

The room has become a club of legend, with numerous luminaries of Hollywood, stage, film and television having frequented the venue many times over the years. The three decades of shows and performers at the club are more than likely in a 'lost count" status, though I believe Tom has kept all the annual performance reservation date books and has them in a safe place, in case the history channel calls for a Chasen's-style documentary. Just considering at one time he did mention that he had an offer some fifteen years ago to have a television show done there, but declined at the time.

It's one of those old style places with the ambience being that of classic and period, not modern, so when you walk into the room it takes you back in time. If you're not initially hip to that, than it may take a little time, but after a great cocktail or two, you'll be fine and fit right in, even if a celebrity icon is sitting at the table next to you, or in my case, the bar, where I've served many who've simply preferred to lounge back in the very comfortable, cushioned raised seats and become unknown, since they've already achieved the opposite. I enjoy serving the disappearing ones.

Holding only 70 people, every seat is basically an orchestra pit. But we can get some persnickety individuals wanting this or that table for various reasons, without realizing that when it's a packed house the choice becomes limited due to the deuces, three and four-tops of reservations that more-less design the seating arrangement so that everyone fits with no seat open and empty. Not an easy thing to do in an L-shaped room. Even the major celebs don't act all that, just the ones of high drama.

If you consider the numbers over this journey of time, we've had well over a thousand singers through the room, and ones that still perform here today into their own decades-long careers.

The art of the intimate performance; it's like saloon singing, but without the high stage. And you never know who's going to be in the audience, so it's always good to hit it out of the ballpark. After entering the club, the eyes adjust to the lighting on low, and the mind is soon transported into your own musical film noir where one can turn into any character they so desire for the night.

The Gardenia is also home to the longest-running open mic night in town, now in its 13th year. This gives newcomers a chance to feel welcomed into the Cabaret community, where they can gain equal footing and confidence to sing their craft and build a show of their own all the while experiencing and hearing other singers, voices and interpretations, a comraderie into the art of the song.

This is the venue where Michael Feinstein got his start, along with

Andrea Marcovicci and Maude Maggart, who's younger sister is Fiona Apple. These are just to note a few of the many. Then you have already established legends like Margaret Whiting who performed at the club many years ago, as well as Julie Wilson, Janis Paige and Neile Adams who've done shows as recent as a couple years ago, and they're in their 70's, 80's and 90's, respectively. You've got to hand it to the gals of old, they just keep on rolling!

Than you have the biggest supporters of the club who live in the area, performers like Tom Culver, Keri Kelsey, Robyn Spangler, Candace J. Hincks, Julie Esposito, Christel Alexander, Pat Whiteman and many others listed on the Gardenia facebook page, not to mention all the club goers who come in to see shows of all kinds who are not performers themselves, as well as ones who work in all the other areas of the entertainment business, but don't do Cabaret. Scotty Bowers and his wife, Lois, have been coming into the club for many years. Scotty, a bartender way before my time and still today, is the author of the recent New York Times Bestseller "Full Service", about his experiences doing what he did in Hollywood for over 50 years.

The one great thing that separates The Gardenia Room from other like-venues across the country is that Tom keeps the club open out of the passion for the art as an environment for new talent to grow. This has to do with his own previous career as a dancer, singer, actor and choreographer on Broadway. He also worked at New York's famous Latin Quarter that was owned by Barbara Walter's father, Lou. Tom has told me many of his stories over the years. Why he hasn't written a book/memoir of his own is beyond me, and I've asked him. We're also the only club of its type that doesn't take a cut of the performer's cover charge. Cabaret is like the nice sister, with Burlesque being its naughty twin!

Though it started out more just as a restaurant for lunch and dinner in the very early years, it included a back patio for afternoon seating. Industry types running businesses in the area would walk down the alley between Sycamore and La Brea and turn right up into Tom's lunch patio. In fact, the original chairs are still corner-stacked up against the fence and brick wall of The Guitar Institute next door, out in what used to be the patio, now weathered by rain and rusted from years of non-use.

Change happens over a length of time, and links to the past can be hard to let go of, when you don't quite want to say goodbye yet. As you get older, memories can seep in deeper in the mellow attempt of holding on to what's already gone. The youth in the mind still remains. Knowing me, I'd be the same way, for building good memories makes for lasting memories later, creating a never-ending smile inside from participating in something historic for the record books. There's a sentimental feeling with being the boy behind the bar at a place of note for so long. When you have the same original owners, and the staff's slow rate of turnover, we all know each other well.

I remember when I first got hired there. It was in 89'or 90'. I was looking for more work in the yellow pages after checking out all the want ads, as I also liked calling establishments that weren't necessarily hiring bartenders at the moment. I lived in Burbank at the time, and drove into Hollywood to fill out an application, not knowing if they could really use me or not. But I had just left a downtown gig that I couldn't stand anymore, on 444 Flower Street right across the way from the Bonaventure Hotel, so I needed to fill my work schedule out as quickly as possible to avoid a financial nosedive and living in my truck.

Tom and I talked, along with his manager at the time, about me actually coming in to start shifting behind the bar with a beginning schedule. So poof, I was in. But what I had gotten into, I had no idea at the time. It was a weird period of adjustment for me at the onset, getting used to the vibe and my place within it. And I had to cool my energy down to fit in to how the room rolled from the beginning to the end, finding my place in the script. Tom was the director, and took a chance on me as the young bar actor. The position carried with it a center of attention as the opening act. It took me awhile, but I learned how to control it and ride the wave to shore.

The reservation books dictate to a large degree of how busy a night is going to be, and they wanted me behind the bar on some slow nights too, of which there was a slight misunderstanding at first until I figured it out, that sometimes included calling in to see if they needed me, or them calling me, as the numbers in the books can and do increase day-by-day up until a performer's show date. I was a newbie to this rare kind of venue in Los Angeles, as anybody would be with this few and far between theme, so it took me a while to adjust to the life of activity in the room before I settled in with everything I needed to be aware of in my overall job description, which included being in charge of the house music and volume, the phones, coffees and waters, and disappearing in the shadows of the bar when the show starts.

One of the odd things that happens every night unlike anywhere else is, when it's show time at 9:00pm, after full seating and dinner and drinks have been completed, the room goes dark except for the stage lights, the bar is dimmed, and I'm the only one left out on the floor (behind the bar) being quiet as a mouse, even to the point when making drinks during the show, all drinks and martinis have to be shaken during the applause so the sound doesn't interrupt the performance, which is why we don't use blenders anymore, too loud for the room no matter what. I like that!

There was one time just a couple years ago when a performer was in the middle of a slow, jazzy medley of songs and the crowd wasn't huge, at the same time I was jammed with a few martini orders from the waiters, so I went outside on the sidewalk of Santa Monica Boulevard and rocked my full bullet martini shaker for a good 15-20 seconds, came back into the club, raised the bar gate, and poured into the already chilled martini glasses.

With all the traffic going by, it's good no squad cars caught me, who knows what would have happened. Imagine me going to jail for preparing cocktails on the street. However, one thing I can say about that is, this part of the boulevard in Hollywood is also part of the last extension of Route 66 that goes all the way to the ocean's edge in Santa Monica. Therefore, I can officially say that I have shaken martinis on Route 66, however late it may be for the history books.

These types of clubs survive on a shoestring more or less, so as a community of like-minded artists, everyone supports each other as much as one can, as it tries to keep a toehold of exposure and recognition in American entertainment. Facebook not only helps get the word out, but images and video content as well. I've been the administrator of the page since it began two years ago. It's funny out of all this time I've never sat in the main room to see a show on an off night. Occasionally when I'm alone in the room early on setting up the bar, I'll turn on the mic and music system and practice belting a few songs just for fun, but I could never do a show.

It all remains a grassroots effort to keep it alive and kicking, an avenue for talent, of which it has in abundance, both new and established, and making money at it as a performer depends on the size of your band. Musicians have to be paid. You have a small room in which to fill up. The only advertising the house does is with the marquee on the boulevard. It's up to the performer to promote. These factors go into the price of your cover charge, all with a prayer that your besties come in to see the show and are not out of town. Most of the time, you're just happy to break even.

But you see all kinds in the world of Cabaret, from super-talented singers who are completely broke and get little to no help or support, to trust-fund performers in a position of living off the money of others, paying for recognition more than earning it, like their own PR person for a media/gossip tabloid. Luckily these are few and far between. And you never want to announce it to the struggling. The one universal centerpiece that doesn't budge – you need to have talent and luck on your side. No other combination works, not even money and nepotism. When executives invest in talent, they count on it for as long a run as they can, so you also have to be professional and intelligent with your craft, and a charming and workable-with personality doesn't hurt either. Though you may be able to buy your way for a while, it's going to be a hard fall back down to the ground if you don't have a wide variety of immensely creative ways to sustain you up at the top, where talent still matters most of the time.

As we continue on with the doors open, Tom decorates the room with flowers, Bruce tunes the piano and changes the performer names on the marquee, Nichole takes care of the floor, bookings and reservations, Leonel handles the kitchen, and I'm on the bar.

Below is a list of celebrities that have graced the room at The Gardenia since I've been there, and that I've served cocktails to:

Clint Eastwood   Ann Margret   Charles Bronson   Tom Bosley

Michael Learned   Annette Bening   Chevy Chase   Gil Gerard

Raquel Welch   Richard Mulligan   Rita Moreno   Henry Jaglom

Carol Channing   Michael Madsen   Natalie Schafer   Tyne Daly

Kevin McCarthy   Charlene Tilton   Stevie Wonder   Ken Berry

Maria Shriver   Henry Mancini   Cheryl Bentyne   Robert Urich

Marcia Wallace   Robert Goulet   Carol Lawrence   Billy Vera

Marion Ross   Michael Feinstein   Nancy Sinatra   Norman Lear

Mel Brooks   Anne Bancroft   Gregory Harrison   Lainie Kazan

Sidney Poitier   Bonnie Franklin   Ron Glass   Phyllis Diller

Martin Landau   Shirley Jones   Bruce Vilanch   Nancy Dussault

Tim Curry   Sally Struthers   Richard Benjamin   Judith Light

Patrick Swayze   Bea Arthur   Nick Cassavetes   Jean Simmons

James Garner   Michelle Lee   Mike Stoller   Carl Reiner

Joanne Worley   Rex Reed   Peri Gilpin   Mr. Blackwell

Peisha McPhee   Leonard Maltin   Sally Kirkland   Gary Collins

Joan Van Ark   Jack Klugman   Barbara Bain   Dick Sherman

Anne Rutherford   Elliot Gould   Carole Cook   James Cromwell

Yvette Mimieux   Karen Morrow   Richard Gautier   Keith David

Melissa Manchester   Ray Evans   Amanda McBroom

Anne Kerry Ford   Robben Ford   Lee Meriwether   Sally Field

Ray Jessel   Fiona Apple   Jason Alexander   Tyrone Power Jr.

Richard Chamberlain   Charlotte Rae   Lawrence Pressman

Leonard Nimoy   Dick Van Patten   Mary Ann Mobley

Betty Garrett   Cloris Leachman   Rob Reiner   Buddy Collette

Peter Gallagher   Pia Zadora   George Chakiris   Jackie Collins

John Glover   Adrienne Barbeau   Michelle Phillips

Bruce Davison   Anne Jeffreys   Frank Strazzeri   Susan Blakely

James Pickens Jr.   Mary Jo Catlett   Sammy Williams

Sally Kellerman   Lesley Ann Warren   Margaret O'Brien

Estelle Getty   Robert Wuhl   Chris Noth   Robert Guilliame

Jim. J. Bullock   Deborah Van Valkenburgh   Lydia Cornell

Beverly Sanders   Alan Mandell   Treisa Gary   Jackaye Harry

19

HIGHLAND TAFFY

When you're on Facebook next time, type in the keywords to a page called "Hidden Los Angeles". It covers very interesting histories on places in town that kind of go unreported and forgotten over time. This is one of those places.

The Highland Taffy Estate, as it is now called, is the old estate built in 1928 that was once owned by William Randolph Hearst. It was actually the first property he bought as his residence shortly after moving to LA. Today, it is now a private residence. The previous owner was architect Henry Lovins, designer of the Pig N' Whistle restaurant, which was originally the concession stand for the Egyptian Theatre.

With a long, narrow gated driveway sitting between a Best Western Hollywood Plaza Inn Motel and the American Legion Hall Post 43 at 2025 N. Highland Avenue, about a quarter-mile south of the Hollywood Bowl, it is an artistic gem of a property, a multi-level landscape with two homes, art studios, lush greenery, and walkways to the top where a small, amphitheatre-style wedding chapel is built up against a mountain wall. This was also the original hideout for Hearst's mistress, the actress Marion Davies. They ended up together for over 30 years.

In talking with the caretaker of the estate, he let me know that one time he had to run off a specific homeless person that was reported to be an ex-scientist PHD intellectual that dropped his once successful life and went completely off the grid. I'm sure there's a sneak trail of open land where homeless people hang out somewhere between Taffy's mountain edge and extends all the way over to the nosebleed section of the Bowl's amphitheatre, free concerts from an easy distance away.

That's what I would do, build the perfect tent area campgrounds in the gap where no one goes – a place to survive and exist in some form, full of individuals who've fallen through the ever-widening cracks in the economic pavement, and geniuses who gave up on the corrupt American system to be truly free with whatever new set of hardships they have to deal with, but having no monthly bills at all, nor an address. Like anything else, it's a trade-off.

Spring to Fall, they rent out the venue location for parties, weddings and other functions. This is how I got in the door, bartending for a caterer who is on their office listing as preferred and recommended foodies. I come along for the providing of the drink.

It was a wedding party for 150 guests. We're allowed to use the kitchen areas of both houses for all the food prep and beverage back-up. There were three bars spread out over the property. At the bottom level bar was veteran actor Casey Sander, who played the character of Wade Swoboda in the TV series *Grace Under Fire*, but has many other film and TV credits to his name. He still loves to get out and tend bar on occasion, as he used to work for years as a bartender at the famous Gladstone's on PCH in Malibu. His talent manager is James Garner's daughter.

At the mid-level bar was commercial, stage, TV and film actor Michael Childers once again, who basically does the same between acting gigs, along with still bartending at the Formosa Café, the only bartender survivor from some newly-implemented bar craft cocktail program, which turned out to be the wrong place to exercise such a culinary demon. Not in a classic, old Hollywood haunt where celebs have been hanging out since the late 20's. Legend has it that Frank Sinatra spent many nights at the Formosa in the 1950's, pining over Ava Gardner. The interior and the exterior of the bar can also be seen in the movie, L.A. Confidential. Across the street is Jones Café, and my Gardenia Room is just a block east from there on the other side of La Brea, all three on Santa Monica Boulevard, that is thankfully cleaned up now from what used to be hooker central a decade ago. I ended up being given the duties at the bar on the top level, which would get hit first after the ceremony ended.

We all arrive in the limited parking area to do a massive crew unload of anything and everything from the company vans. Michael and I have our gloves on to avoid any nicks and scuffs before we actually get to setting up the bars, nice-looking hands behind the bar is always a good thing. Getting a bleeder is never something to look forward to. But I have various sizes of band-aids in a Ziploc baggie in my kit for the little emergencies.

I see some of the new cocktailian bartenders on my Facebook page who will go as far as to announce when they nearly slice their thumb off to the point of a dozen stitches, and for the next two weeks they're wearing finger condoms, which don't allow for the best air-breathing for healing purposes, along with extra-caution hand movements all because a slip of the blade while more than likely looking the other way when someone harks their name on a busy night.

When you're cutting fruit, pay attention to nothing else until it's done. I prefer a knife with a serrated edge so it can catch its own fall, as opposed to a smooth blade all the way to the tip. You're dealing with all kinds of fruits with an equal amount of different skins, some easy, some tough. Working the cut through is sometimes safer than becoming lazy about it with too much ease. But the initial key – Keep the hands and fruit dry. Slippage is too common. And know your knife. It isn't worth losing any work over, or feeling the throb of blood pressure in the finger when you do work. But this is what happens when you cut fresh throughout a shift with the huge range of garnishes they use in today's craft bars, instead of what you think you'll use for the night beforehand. This, I can do, because I know in advance how busy I'm going to be. Bars, on the other hand, some nights of the week you just don't know.

After all the set-up, we have about forty-five minutes to shift our vehicles into the huge back parking lot next door at the Legion, freshen ourselves up from the sweat break and change into our formal attire. Michael borrows my lint roller while I put on my cologne, and then we have a smoke and shoot the shit of our lives for awhile until we cruise back in for any early guest arrivals. It's nice just to get back behind the bar and relax our faces into happy mode. Sometimes we have a pop, sometimes we don't, all depends on how we feel at the moment, if anything is bothering us to where we need to arc it up a notch.

It was a beautiful day, but very warm during the top of the afternoon. We always look forward to when the sun dips down slightly below the mountain ridge and we get the evening shade that cools the pores for the rest of the night while we're slinging away. It gets busy with easy drinks at the onset as most don't want to get plastered before the ceremony. The initial pre-ceremony reception lasts a little over an hour with some light appetizers passed. With an acoustic guitar and violin singing through the air, the rest of the band sets up as eventually all of the guests are requested to head their way to the chapel above.

It was a good rush for all of us when you get hit with 150 thirsty travelers in time. Not too many repeat offenders, mostly quenchers coming back for mineral or still waters. It's re-stocking hour, and managing the 40 lb. ice bags to hold us down till the end without everything melting away. The ceremony lasts 30-45 minutes and then we're back at it again, this time with more regular drinking of the spirits, classic cocktails, wines, beers and champagne. I even make a few blast from the past Long Island Teas along with Drivers, Hounds, Cape's, and hey, the Cosmo is still in fashion – which is basically nothing more than a Kamikaze with a dash of cranberry juice, but chilled straight up in a martini glass instead of as a cold shot or on-the-rocks. Plus I always make something special with what I have to work with, stock-wise, behind the bar, just to make it interesting for myself. If I have peach schnapps, lemonade and pomegranate, I can play that into a few different drinks, but sometimes the pickings are slim.

And Mojitos are always a bitch to prepare outside, because the mint dies in the heat pretty quick. They're better left in the cooler-frig of a bar where they can keep crisp and its aromatic essence alive. Otherwise, at a party this size, if one guest orders a Mojito, it usually starts an avalanche of everybody wanting one out of trend, without realizing each one is made from scratch, taking longer, yet still failing its desired effect because it's best if everything going into the glass is cold, meaning the rum and club soda too. The mint, lime and sugar is what it is, but this is outdoors, so if the mint is warm, sweaty and getting limp by the hour, this is where you lose, by taking all that time stress-prepping them with a less than excellent result, while you still have a line at the bar that really should have been avoided in the first place. If it's a party of 50, than it's approachable, but not 150 people. You can use any of the various Mojito mixers on the market, but it's still not the real deal, and takes about the same amount of time because you're still muddling the mint if you have it there. I do love having mint as a garnish though, and it smells nice around the bar when a big bag of it is open.

The waiter captain is making sure plenty of guests go to the other bars for drinks to help spread it out and share the duties, but it also helps the guests in knowing all the walkways to explore while they're on the property. A long buffet is set-up for dinner at the tables, and the band is playing some good, deep jazz with great vocals from a singer who really knows the old American songbook. We get to the past-rush point at the bars where it's more relaxed after knocking back a few with everybody's liquid tanks getting filled up. Time to catch up with ice refill once again and clear any mess created while pouring and shaking on-the-fly. I like the pace and challenge to kick ass in high gear, but it's also nice when it cools down where I can cruise out the rest of the night, allowing for more customer interaction, which is a good thing. The guests enjoy some chat at the bar, and so do I. A chance to relate with someone you've never met before and you'll probably never see again - in through the outdoor.

I think about all the history of the estate while I have moments behind the bar, panning around and knowing what it looks like in both the day and the night with lights and long candles, along with walking the landscape as much as I had time for. I wonder how many secrets went to the grave, if the houses are haunted, or any apparitions in the dark of night. As I spoke of Culver Studios in the previous story "Quiet on the Set", the President and Founder of the studios, silent movie pioneer and "Father of the Western", Thomas Ince, was invited to a party of his 42nd birthday in his honor, on Hearst's yacht in 1924. He never made it off alive.

The story goes is that Hearst was jealous thinking that Charlie Chaplin went off to another part of the yacht with Marion Davies. When he caught up with them, Hearst had a gun and shots were being fired willy-nilly. As the two were speaking, the man turned around and Hearst accidentally shot him in the chest. But it wasn't Chaplin, it was Ince. After his mysterious death aboard the yacht, that was also alleged that he had not been shot, just had bad stomach indigestion and heart trouble, the studio was then purchased by producer/director, Cecil B. DeMille. There are several versions of the big cover-up.

Feeling so bad, rumor had it that Hearst paid off Ince's widow's mortgage on the Chateau Elysee apartment building in Hollywood (now the Church of Scientology Celebrity Centre that I mentioned in the previous story "Party of 8"), as well as providing her with a trust fund just before she left for Europe. In turn, she refused an autopsy and ordered her husband's immediate cremation.

The Chateau was originally built as a replica of a 17th Century French-Normandy castle, and ran as a residential apartment house by Ince's widow, Elinor, for up and coming movie stars. But it operated like a hotel with daily maid service and meals served out of a formal dining room. Some of the many famous residents of the 30's and 40's were Bette Davis, Clark Gable, Errol Flynn, Edward G. Robinson, Carol Lombard, Ginger Rogers, Humphrey Bogart, Lillian Gish, George Gershwin, and Ed Sullivan. It became known as The Manor.

Shortly after, in 1928, RKO acquired the studios and controlled it for years, bringing stardom to many legends, including Bette Davis, Cary Grant, Katherine Hepburn, Robert Mitchum, Fred Astaire and Ginger Rogers. Later in 1940, it was reported that stagehands high in the catwalks were confronted by a ghostly figure resembling Thomas Ince. How's that for coming back to haunt you? He must've been pissed. And if he could be seen there, I don't see a reason why he couldn't have made it over to the Highland Taffy to spook Hearst out of his bed. In 1950, Howard Hughes acquired RKO Pictures, and in 1956, after Lucille Ball didn't a get the leading role in a major movie that she wanted badly, she was so mad that her and Desi Arnaz purchased the lot and made it Desilu Productions.

As a side note, Scotty Bowers, author of the 2012 New York Times bestseller "Full Service", whom I've known for years from him coming into The Gardenia Room, went to one of Hearst's parties at the castle up in San Simeon, California in the 40's, shortly after coming home from military service in WWII. Scotty may very well be the only person alive today that ever attended one of the those parties.

The thought of Marion Davies comes back to my mind with her living on the property. She was such a good soul, yet in a strange situation that she just rode out to the end until Hearst died in 1951. The night before his death, there had been a lot of people in the house. Marion was very upset by the large crowd of family and friends. She said it was too noisy and were disturbing Hearst, who was ill in bed, by talking so loud. She was upset and had to be sedated. When she woke, her niece, Patricia Van Cleve Lake, and her husband, Arthur Lake, told her that Hearst was dead, and that his lawyer's associates had removed his body as well as all his belongings and any trace that he had lived there with her. Marion was banned from Hearst's funeral. Upon Patricia's death, it was revealed she had been the love child of Davies and Hearst.

In addition to her acting career, she spent much of her time at Cosmopolitan Pictures as a production manager. She had been appointed to this position by Hearst, who wanted to keep her close to him. She had a long-standing reputation in the film industry for being extremely kind to the casts and crews of her films, going so far as to pay hospital bills anonymously if she heard that they were ill. She was famous for doing dead-on impersonations of celebrities at parties. And being the practical joker, she once got President Calvin Coolidge drunk by feeding him wine and telling him it was fruit juice. When Davies was in England, she learned that forgotten silent actress Florence Turner, who had been a star at Vitagraph, was destitute. A compassionate Davies paid for her and her mother to return to the U.S., put them up in a hotel, and offered Turner a job with her production company.

Marion started lots of charities including a children's clinic. She was very generous and was loved by everyone who knew her. She died 10 years later, in 1961, in Hollywood. Marion is interred at Hollywood Memorial Cemetery (now called Hollywood Forever), in section B, east side of the lake very close to the grave of Tyrone Power. This cemetery, by the way, in the summer, shows full-length feature film screenings outdoors on the property on weekends. A different kind of drive-in, among many of Tinsletown's resting celebrities, showing the movies projected onto a mausoleum's white marble wall. They also have DJ's spinning music before and after the film. It's called Cinespia. Check them out at Cinespia.org. for a calendar of screenings.

It's that time of the night after plenty of dancing and drinking, and things are slowly coming to a close. We all start fading things out of whatever's left that hasn't been consumed and emptied. During a long shift, packing up at the end on a 4-tier property like this is a little more on the strain than we'd care to admit. But we do it as the finish line is near. I chat with the caretaker one more time before we call it a night. He's a great guy and loves the property, so you know it's being well taken care of until the next time we get the call to come over and do it all again.

20

CHELSEA BEHAVING BADLY

Punked is the only word I can come up with what happened, or at least what it ended up to be after the smoke cleared.

Back in 2004 I was working all over at the time, a couple years after I left Lakeside, including gigs at the Palladium. One of the bartenders I worked with often there was Marie, who was a regular combination of angel and devil. So each time behind the bar with her could either be fun or a scene of sensitive communication during the shift. My goal – keep her in a good mood and enjoy her great breasts whenever she brushed them by my upper arms back and forth while getting draught beers, which was usually on my side, strategically speaking!

The easier I made it for her, the better. She was like a tough, sexy street girl with some incarnation of badass, combined with a bit too much pull towards religion and politics going on in her head, all the while being another struggling actor in Hollywood. Let's just say that with questions of attitude, getting along has a lot to do with making it in Tinseltown. And still being a rebellion in your late 40's doesn't quite cut it for the temperance that needs to be practiced to have success in the big picture, and a shit load of quality connections built up over years.

Some people are more comfortable remaining stubborn instead of embracing change, as though they have something in a dark past to uphold and drag around like a ball and chain, of which most of us have at some point or another in our lives until we just say "Fuck it, I'm Me". But this surrendering of "I can't carry it anymore" is exactly what's needed to slowly ease the hold and let things go. To forgive, to apologize, and say goodbye to weighty, negative things of all kinds so they fall away to the past, where they belong. Forward out of the cave is forward, and that direction is a one-way.

I remember for some time trying to help her with what she even admits and acknowledges about herself, of which I admired and respected about her, as we had fun together too, Marie had a nice side as well, it was just the stern edge of an undercurrent that needed to disappear. But it could sustain brutal outcomes at times when it wasn't necessarily called for.

I get a call from her one day in the middle of the week, asking me if I want to tend bar with her at a gallery showing in the Artist's District of Santa Monica. It was just for a few 3-4 short hours. My minimum is usually 5 hours. I had to think about it for a minute, because if another gig came up for the same date where I'd make more money, then I'd be stuck. Luckily it was on a Thursday evening, lessening the chance of a double-booking, so I went ahead and confirmed to do it with her. The money was okay enough to make the trek over the hill from the valley, taking Topanga Canyon through to Pacific Coast Highway, then PCH to Santa Monica, avoiding the 405 freeway altogether.

Our friendship/relationship was that of a title from the Led Zeppelin song "Good Times, Bad Times". The day of the event she calls to let me know that something came up on her end and she wasn't going to be able to do the event with me. She mentioned there was a replacement for her, so I would be walking into another mystery gig hoping all would go well, with or without Marie there.

I arrive in the parking lot early, so I hung out listening to Tom Leykus on the radio while I smoked a cig and got my bar kit ready to schlep over my shoulder, yet once again. Walking into the building with first eyes on where the bar was set-up, I introduced myself to someone that looked like they might know what was going on. The lady, named Chelsea, than introduced me to the other bartender, Melissa. She was a nice, young cute girl with I'm guessing some Filipino in her. I get there to find out the bar was limited to select wines and micro brews and just a few choice spirits, sodas and juices, making it easier and quicker to throw together in ready mode.

Soon I found myself standing around for a while before guest arrivals of the artsy type, kind of up my alley actually, except for the potential snob factor. Then all the sudden I began over-hearing a distant but audible freak out session happening in the back room. Chelsea in charge came out and was heading directly towards me. Where's my disappearance switch when I needed it?

Face-to-face, she told me an artist was not going to make it in with a final painting to fill a big, open naked spot on the wall that I could see from the bar clear as day. The question followed:

Chelsea: Kyle, I have a big favor to ask of you, have you ever painted before ?

Me: No, not really, but I have an artistic background with other things I've done.

Chelsea: Well, I have a 24x36 canvas in the backroom with someone's color palate of paint and a couple brushes. Can you fill it up with something/anything will do, just so I can hang a piece in that spot for now until the showing is over. We only have about 20 minutes. Can you please, please do this for me?

Me: Ahh, ugh, yeah, umm, I'll do what I can for you. Bring out the stuff so I can see what I have to work with.

Chelsea: Oh, thank you, thank you so much, you're a lifesaver.

Touching my shoulder, she walked away to the back room to gather what was needed. I went to work, quietly, but ever curiously. Intuition works best in those with free, silent minds, and something was knocking that door, a signal trying to come in, while I was occupied with the acceptance of this impromptu task at hand. Whenever I commit to doing something, I prefer to get to the finish line if I'm going to put the time in at all. This painting was no different. It was a bang-it-out job, that's all, a piece in an overall wall puzzle to fill a void. But still, I tried to do something special with it, given what I'm given to work with – life's designed limitations !

I mean, how much heart could one put into the art with less than a half hour to work with. It's not like I was commissioned or anything. But effort is effort, however racing the pace was. With the colors I had to work with, the end result was like a sky blue inner-outer background with

white clouds peaking through, centered more or less with yellows, greens and reds, orange and browns, like tulips in a spring wind or a chili pepper soiree. I wasn't going for that or anything in particular, just following where it was taking me. It's interesting to paint with nothing in mind, little care, not much concern, but you don't want to produce total shit either. I was just hoping for a passable piece that I wouldn't turn away looking at it myself, once it was mounted next to the real works of art.

So I thought . . .

Chelsea came out of the back room as I was finishing up, though with a painting, it never really feels done. It can be endlessly tinkered with until you run the possibility of screwing it up altogether, where you scrap it and start all over. But I didn't have that luxury. There is a point moment when you have to drop the brush and let it dry, surrendering to whatever is.

The Artist's Life Nightmare – The suffering for perfection while attempting to settle for excellence. Most people would love this life

. . . but as a leisure hobby . . . not to survive off of it.

I clean my hands and get back to the bar. Chelsea takes the easel and materials in back and has the painting hung on the wall just in time for the doors.

Melissa arrived back behind the bar that I really preferred to work alone since Marie made a clean exit elsewhere, so we engaged in some mild conversation sharing the same space, but you can't create your own individual vibe of presence as much when working alongside another, especially a rookie stranger from another generation. This always leads to several "get me out of here" moments, but I do my best to maintain a sense of professionalism that others around can be oblivious to position or concern. It made me curious of her in the form of further investigative observance while I was there on location.

Guests arrive like a slow, staggered platoon getting dropped off by a bus. A line had gathered outside unnoticeable from the inside with the glass of the door's tinted. Greeting and drinking took its first turn around, and after the initial rush to the hosted spirits, you then become the casual observer of event activity, like the suited bald guys in Fringe. With the guest count of this event, I could have worked the bar solo, but since there were two of us, it made it easier. Too easy! Melissa was cool, but I was also happy when she would leave the bar for short periods. Otherwise, the time would go by slower.

The discipline of an enlightened master lacking need or initiated interest to speak at all – internal peace in the middle of chaos, serving with the kind silence of responding gestures instead of words.

The walls get busy with eyes gazing at the works from the various artists. The petite femme fatale hip-hugging me, nudges and points with surprise as a few gallery goers hover and chat with Chelsea around and underneath my freshly-fucked painting. She is there to sell and make a commission. Her motivation was strong. Though a humorous grin peeked at the possibility, I didn't take it seriously at all. And then it all changed into the high drama nightmare.

A couple minutes go by after some happy commotion at a distance, and Melissa decides to walk over and catch Chelsea as she was walking to the back. She comes back to me with the news. Out of all the art work, Chelsea sold my painting first, for $10,000. Hard bargain to swallow, much less believe. I stood and watched it play out but was too far away to hear specific words. I asked myself "Had it even fully dried yet?" My bar girl was curious of my stoic stance, and then says to me "You know, she plans on keeping it all for herself, including your commission, and giving you nothing". "Really" I said "I didn't know I was supposed to get something . . . though I wouldn't say no to receiving" But all the evidence wasn't in yet.

When Chelsea came to the bar with a frontal assault of the sale, that's when my passive shifted to aggressive. When something is put in your face like that, you may as well bark and defend, hell, it's almost being requested of me. Delivering with no armor, I engaged in a verbal joust with Chelsea that started with medium body, all the while Melissa was standing there offering encouragement for what she thought was rightfully mine, a cut fair and square. Chelsea played it off like a shark clamping to the money bone, happy with her expanded chunk, sufficient with her reasoning, than slowly walked away with the guilty smile of a bitch in high gear.

With the entire crowd of invitees hanging out and talking amongst themselves over art, drinking and eyeing plates of finger food not in arms reach, I walked out from behind the bar and went to the center of the main floor in the open room, and proceeded with getting everyone's attention for a minute.

Watching Chelsea's jaw drop from the corner of my eye was sweet to behold, at the same time I sent Melissa into OMG! Status as she stood behind the bar alone. Out loud it poured from me.

"Can I get everyone's attention for a minute, please . . . thank you .

. . Hello, my name is Kyle, I've been tending bar for you this evening. I wanted to let you all know what just happened here. Before you arrived, I helped the host of this gallery showing . . . I'm sure you all know her, she's right there. She was in a jam with an artist not showing up with a painting to fill a space on the wall. I painted a canvas on-the-fly for her. Well, that painting sold just a few minutes ago for $10,000. That's not the problem, though. The issue is to let you know that she plans on keeping all the money, instead of just her commission, so as the artist, I get nothing for helping her out in a pinch. I don't know how you feel about that, but I thought it only fair to let you know. I'll leave it up to you to decide . . . but I feel I should get something. Thanks"

I walk back to the bar and stand next to Melissa. A couple minutes later, a slew of once invisible crew walk over to the bar, including Chelsea, to let me know in no silent treatment "Kyle, you've just been pranked on Girls Behaving Badly!" That's when I just put my arms in the air, walked out from the bar and surrendered with relief and laughter.

Getting punked didn't bother me nearly as much as knowing that Marie made money off of it, while she was gone as a participant from a distance. She got a good laugh at my expense. But over the years, I took that money and more back out of her pocket in ways she doesn't even know about to this day. She's one of those individuals that can dish it, but can't take it. There are some times where an eye-for-an-eye is fitting punishment as return volley. Knowing Marie and her capability for vengeance, if I would have done such a thing, her head would have exploded in anger like a scene from Scanners.

The whole time, I was on the fence with taking all this as being real and true, than knowing at a certain stage of the evening that it couldn't have been, which is why I made my final curtain call at the end in an attempt to even the score, just in case. I had nothing to lose at that point.

Months later, I was contacting them to get a VHS copy of the segment or episode for myself, but I can only pull teeth for so long. Eventually, it showed up in the mail. I shoved it into the player just to find out that whoever the editor was cut out the good stuff and made me look like an ass instead. I never watched their program, so maybe that was simply par for what they do. It could have been, in my opinion, so much better entertainment, but they weren't about to air my grandstanding of turning the table and calling Chelsea out.

Oh, by the way, the then Chelsea I'm speaking of . . . is the now famous Chelsea Handler.

One final note. I did end up getting the painting as a parting gift. I have it in the garage at home.

21

THE SICILIAN CONNECTION

In 1995, I was called and asked by Tony, one of the Bellissimo brothers, to come and work his bar at the Café Bellissimo in Thousand Oaks, off of Moorpark Road and 101 freeway. It was a great building and property along with the interior, and with its volume potential, I couldn't say no.

However, it did require me to drive 15 miles to work as opposed to just walking to work at the original Café B on Ventura Boulevard near my home in Woodland Hills, between Shoup and Fallbrook avenues. I've only been in three situational proximities of walking or riding my bike to work in 30 years, and when you live in L.A., not having to drive everywhere is a sweet thing, and not easy to give up.

But my truck was young then, and with the opportunity to make more money as bartender and bar manager, it had to be a yes. It also had easy parking in back which is something I always pay attention to, not like Hollywood where it costs you and then you still worry and pray it doesn't get broken into after hours when you get out after 3:00am. I have a phobia about that because my truck has been vandalized five times, but has never been stolen. I prefer to keep it that way.

Of course, this meant having to go back to doing inventory and ordering of all the bar product, like I had done at other gigs in the past where I handled both roles, and once again created my own inventory sheets to make it as easy and quick as possible. But I also wanted to help Tony out with putting it all together, from the bar end.

We took over a pre-existing restaurant establishment, so the bar was already in place, it just had to be cleaned thoroughly in and out along with re-arranged placement of certain things; bottles, glassware and all cooler stock with more efficiency of expectation, especially with an occupancy rate of close to 200, plus eight seats at the bar, serving food along with drink as well. Luckily, the kitchen and bar were only separated by a wall, making it close to get to, drop off an order, and get back in rhythm.

We even had a wine cuvee to make by the glass easier/quicker to pour with less moves involved. It was a 4+2 model, chilled for white wine and room temp for red wine. It was mainly designed for 750ml bottles, but I was able to find a way to extend the tube-in-bottle by fitting a certain inch-length of clear plastic tubing on the end of the cuvee's main tube for 1.5 Liter bottles, as it would make it all the way down to the inside bottom of the bottle, making each bottle last twice as long before it had to be changed.

One of the top focuses for Tony was to assemble the waiter talent. After all, this was a singing-server restaurant, just like the original one I started at in Woodland Hills the year before, 1994. So the job description was of dual task, yet of equal importance. With many auditions, things started taking shape. I on the other hand, was not required to hit the stage. It was more of an option.

And we had a centered stage in the main room. It wasn't off in some corner of the floor plan. As part of the audio for the sound system, Tony acquired this special rack CD component with many features, including one that would remove the lead vocal track on any music CD you put into it. This made it so the waiters/singing servers didn't have to rely on or be limited to the use of cassette tapes from those mini-mall karaoke stores. You don't want talent hindered by a watered-down musical cheese version when you could have the real deal sound production instead. Tony paid his ASCAP entertainment fees, so why not!

We don't know where he got the machine, but it was a brilliant move and allowed for the ultimate in flexibility with musical choice and range. My guess is it had to have been a high-end special order from out of the country, that no one knew he had, as there was no way to tell just by looking at it. You had to actually utilize the component's functions by finger to know, of which we did.

Along with all of this, we had a variety of musician accompaniment almost every night of the week. I remember Alan who used to be the touring guitarist with Johnny Rivers, the retired fireman, the major band side player we had, Johnny our Harley-riding acoustic singer, and the regular musician that was at Café B in Woodland Hills, who pulled double-duty at our place initially to start things off when we opened. These were guys who could play and sing a wide swath of music real well.

Tony was our leader and became one of the showmen too. This period of time was back when (okay brace yourself as this might hurt a little bit or make you throw up in your mouth) the "Macarena" was hugely popular. So along with singing "That's Amore" and other good guy favorites like "New York, New York", Tony also took the reign almost every night and nailed the "Macarena" to the wall. Every once in a while early on in the song's worldwide rise to fame we'd all catch one another clapping and singing to the song, then the waiters and I would go into a temporary hiding in back for a minute until the tune was over realizing what we had done.

If you hear a song like this too many times, of which by the way followed the heels of the whole country line-dancing craze that I had just left with Denim & Diamonds, hundreds over the course of a year, it's very possible one may have to enter a mental institution for an undetermined length of time for what could only be termed as an audio exorcism. Even today, if by sheer strange occurrence I hear it blasting out of some distant loudspeaker or broken boombox, I find myself saying "No, no, please, please don't, I can't listen to this, no really, I'm serious", all the while forming a crucifix with my fingers and pulling my beanie down over my ears like a dog hearing an endless siren or some high-pitch freakout. Bringing up that memory from the archive feels like it will never go away. Yes, the "Macarena" burnout was that bad!

The place got cleaned up inside and out, the kitchen crew were put into place and trained on the menu, and everything seemed to be in place. The wine selection was finalized for both glass and bottle, along with popular domestic micro-brews of the time, and the basic spirits that fit the bill, nothing fancy, product that moved, not sitting around gathering dust on an upper shelf for six years. And this was Italian/Sicilian food, so the wines didn't have to be super high-end to be good and acceptable, like one might expect in a fine-dining establishment. Café B had an old-world style and charm to it that only the original owners, Tony and Emilio, could duplicate. It was family oriented, therefore avoiding stuffiness in trade for all to have a good time.

There was even an older couple who worked at both Café B's, where the husband created balloon animals for the kids, while the wife was a palm reader who had a table just inside the front entrance of the restaurant, for customers who were waiting for a table to open. So with this carnie meets the supernatural within the walls topped with live entertainment, a magical suspension of belief had been created, like a stationary traveling circus that never left, intoxicating and addictive. For a couple hours we would take the mind away from all life's troubles, like walking into an improv movie musical that lasted for six hours a night and having dinner in the middle of it while it was being shot.

At its busiest period, it was crazy and chaotic, a runaway train where everyone got caught up in the emotions of the good and bad of what happens on any given shift, even some of the customers.

About a year after we had opened, Tony had got underway with a major wraparound outdoor patio construction that turned out gorgeous when it was completed, and added even more seating and volume to the business. It was a lot to handle for me as one bartender when it was packed, like a heated race to get to the finish line. The rotation of glassware, ice fills, all the drinks from over the bar and all of the waiters, product preps, fruit stock, food orders, it was nuts. Sangria preparation also came in later on with Tony's nephew, Luigi, who put a large batch concoction together, that was very tasty. I still use that recipe today whenever I have a need.

The waiters – Jerry, Michelle, Camille, Zamora, Christine, Matt, Amy, Daniel, Stephanie, Georgina – were a great collection of singing interests with some incredible voices. There were others during that whole stretch of business, but one can only remember so many names. Jerry was the Neil Diamond king, Michelle sang sweet songs and movie themes, Camille was already an impersonator doing Cher, Carmen Miranda, Liza Minnelli, Ethel Merman, and Marilyn Monroe for birthdays. Amy was a young, great blues singer, Stephanie was a musical theatre major, Daniel sang in a variety of genres, Christine and Zamora sang classic rock and pop tunes, Georgina was pop and Broadway, and Matt was a legitimate operatic tenor who wowed everybody. Matt and Stephanie did "The Phantom of the Opera" to some amazing applause.

After it bleeding on me enough, I finally started to get into it as well. I knew I had a good shower voice, but never pursued it before. This was the perfect avenue to enter and sweat it out till I got it right. It took a while to lose most of the shakes, but then I gained more confidence, which then helped my voice relax. I just had to stay with it, but I had the best support and instruction around me so, it was the best of both worlds, singing on the job!

Eventually, after doing many songs solo with just a guitar or piano to accompany me or the use of my own music CD's, I was asked to perform duos and songs with multiple harmonies, which I found was very natural for me. With Christine, I did "Leather and Lace", with Matt and Alan we did a three-part harmony to "Helplessly Hoping" by Crosby, Stills and Nash, A bunch of us guys got up and shared verses and harmony to Don McLean's "American Pie", and I ended up singing lead in a five-part harmony to the Eagles "Best of My Love". Zamora and I performed "More Than Words" by Extreme, Alan and I performed an acoustic version of the Who's "Behind Blue Eyes" with him on guitar and me on vocals, and I sang Poco's "Crazy Love" with the fireman's four-piece band. On my own, I went in a jazz direction with Michael Franks and Charlie Watts Quintet, the British pop/rock of Paul Weller, as well as Journey, Kansas, Boz Scaggs, Lyle Lovett, Stone Temple Pilots, Dan Fogelberg, and the Doobie Brothers. My musical choices were all over the place. I was good with variety. It was great fun. But memorizing lyrics was a bitch, some easier than others. It would usually take me a half-dozen times singing the song before I got it down, yet if you don't sing a certain tune for awhile, one could slip and forget a line. I sing here and there today with a lot of new songs that I jam on that weren't out sixteen years ago, and I still sound fine in the shower, where steam on the throat and vocal chords is the best medicine.

Tammy and Travis were our young seating hosts, and they both got up to sing at some point too. Travis was a hilarious and really smart kid. Him and I would play lounge lizards behind the counter when nobody was looking, putting our own lyrics into songs. He also had this short dancing jig that he would do once in a while that was off the wall, yielding gut-wrenching laughs from all of us watching. I wanted him to do it on the stage to a banjo song from the soundtrack of the movie Deliverance, but the moment was never found. We had our jobs to do. It was crazy!

There were a couple stretches of time during those four years I was there where I was gone for a few weeks at a time. One was for three weeks when I took a temporary acting and touring gig as the set-up man and referee in a Foxy Boxing and Oil Wrestling show with a friend of mine, Dave Robinson, who was both the Emcee and tour lead for a company out of L.A., where he would do this a few times a year for awhile. We basically had 15 shows in 18 days that started in Wyoming and ended up in Pennsylvania before we headed home. It was interesting doing these shows in states like Colorado, Kansas, Oklahoma and Indiana. I was also the night driver. We were in a big, long van with him and I and the four gorgeous girls towing a U-Haul filled with equipment. One of them was supposedly an ex-wife of original member and guitarist of the band Heart, Howard Leese. I never really investigated as to its truth, but she was a very beautiful woman.

Most of the places we were booked in were not fabulous. They were bars and clubs, some seedy, some not so, but they all felt like strange environments when you're there for a one-off show and then you're gone to the next. In the ring, I would referee the girls boxing in sexy outfits they would wear, and even less so with the oil wrestling. I remember being clocked in the face a couple times with the girl's misguided punches. Though the gloves were soft, it didn't necessarily feel that way when it clobbered your jaw. Guys would pay to get in and wrestle with them, and they had a bidding contest, it was nice entertainment and borderline sleazy as you would expect.

The ex-wife and I chatted on the tour and I remember her and I going to have breakfast one time at a restaurant nearby after we arrived in the early morning snow of Colorado to do the first of three shows in two different towns. One night during a show, I was on the outside of the wrestling ring leaning down and sort of officiating but staying out of the way, she had snuck over to the corner on her knees when I wasn't looking. I turned around and she plopped a big, juicy kiss right on my lips. That's what I get for not paying attention. I should be aloof more often! It probably wasn't the best thing for her to do in front of an audience, and it didn't continue on.

But it was all in fun, it was a good show, and we all made decent money, had hotel rooms and food so, I just said what the fuck and went for it, got paid to see some of the country, and was exhausted when I got back. The road home back across the country was a long one. I didn't mess around with the girls, as much as the appetite may have been there. Opportunities presented themselves on a few occasions, but it was best to keep it clean, in case I wanted to go on another tour in the near distance, I didn't want the word to get out to the wrong person and get nixed from any future consideration, possibly without me even knowing.

The other time I was gone from Café B was that of an emergency. I was getting ready to go to work at the restaurant, it was a Friday in July, and a few minutes before I was going to leave the house, I got this collapsing pain in my side that wouldn't go away. I was in great shape and had no idea what was going on. I called work and rushed to the emergency room with the aid of a friend, it was impossible for me to drive. They sedated my pain and started doing tests, finding out far after that it wasn't my appendix, but a couple polyps had perforated in my colon. They were leaking out. I had Diverticulitis, which is an acute case of Diverticulosis. But they didn't know or diagnose that at first.

Early the next day I was on the operating table for what I thought at the time was going to be a couple days in then outpatient. I woke up from what ended up being a 6-hour surgery to find out that they had to do an exploratory repair job. Luckily it was in the ascending section that they could sew up and put me back together without leaving any skin and tube holes open. I was in for seven days with no food, no drink, and no sleep due to that nasty NG tube being so incredibly uncomfortable through the nose and down my throat. I had tubes and vein lines everywhere, even in a place I would have never guessed as necessary. And that was all too creepy getting pulled out!

I had lost 20 pounds of weight that I couldn't afford to have removed from my body, when I barely had any fat percentage to begin with. It was brutal and exhausting, not to mention the morphine giving me hallucinations in the middle of the nights from no silence and peace in the rooms with the nurses and intercom system calling doctors through the ceiling speakers in the hallways. All I wanted was "shut the door and turn off the lights". The first couple days after surgery the morphine drip made me feel "More Fine", but during day three I had to cut it loose and get off it. It was getting me too numb and a bit dreary. After all, it was morphine for pain, not pleasure.

When I got home, I had to eat very easy foods to digest, though I was hungry as a horse. I had to really teach myself again. Now I have a nice big zipper in the middle of my stomach, along with the one they cut for the appendix. I got the 2 for 1 special! All is good though, with my internal engine running even better than before. That's what happens when you get cleaned out and overhauled at the same time as the cut, remove and sew, or as the doctors called it, a dissection. It was three weeks before I got back to work, nice to return and resume the normal activities in my life again. Everybody was wondering what the fuck happened to me. It was too debilitating of a situation in the hospital bed to have visitors other than my mother. So I filled them all in on the medical details and drama with the doctors mandatory "Filet of Kyle" final report in short form and got it over with.

For the next couple years the restaurant stayed nice and busy, packed on the weekends, and our first couple New Years Eves were sold out, as well as other holidays. We developed a lot of regulars that loved coming in just for drinks and appetizers and to see the musical entertainment, as every night it was a little different with something new. And no cover charge at the door.

One of the regulars was this older guy who came in early after we opened and sat at the bar. We got to know each other over a period of time, and he eventually let me know that he was retired CIA agent, spending half of his career time in and out of South America. I didn't make it a point to inquire too deeply, but did make him aware that I was intrigued and was hoping to hear more. He mentioned a couple assignments he had in the past and went into a little detail. He noticed my keen observation skills as a natural, and mentioned that if I was ever interested in becoming an agent, I would have to learn three specific other languages – Russian, Gaelic, and one other that still eludes my memory today, but it very well could be Spanish. One other strange piece of Intel he told me was that in the Thousand Oaks and surrounding area, where the restaurant is located, had the most densely populated group of retired CIA agents and retired MOB bosses than anywhere else in the country. It's hard to ever find out if that's a true fact, but given the mostly beautiful weather year-round, I wouldn't be surprised. I guess they still keep an eye on each other. And there I was, working in a Sicilian restaurant!

Dr. Laura Schlesinger was a regular at the Café B in Woodland Hills, and when Tony opened up ours in Thousand Oaks, her and her husband came out to dine there too on occasion. And the parents of Ron Goldman (O.J. Simpson murder case) came in once in a while after that whole legal debacle and the terrible loss of their son. That crime happened in 1994, just a year before the Thousand Oaks Café B got going. So hard to believe it's been almost 20 years already since that horrific tragedy.

All in all, we had a lot of fun during the time of the restaurant's existence. But by 1998, business volume started to tail off at a concerned degree. The prices got hiked with some of the dinners on the menu a couple times in that last year, and I started to see the writing on the wall that maybe it was time to move on. Tony's girlfriend, who would sometimes sit at the bar and have a glass of wine, mentioned to me that she heard that the nightclub Provence, on the property of the Westlake Inn was looking for a bar manager. So I went over there to Human Resources and put a resume in. I was called in for an interview within the following few days, got the job, and gave my two-week notice to Café B. The plus is that it was five miles closer to home. The minus is that I had to get used to putting in 50-hour work weeks, on an acceptable salary. Initially, I was just happy to make a smooth, quick transition from one job to the next, and thankful to the boss' girlfriend for the tip and hookup.

I worked with the Café B family for close to five years in total, along with picking up other bar work whenever Tom needed me at The Gardenia on nights I had off. But this is how it goes in the business. Establishments rise and fall. So I always have to keep an eye and ear open for when it's time to make that shift whenever it comes around and shows itself as a necessary next move. There are some places of work where you really don't want to leave, but you also need to avoid getting caught under the bridge too.

It was a good run . . .

22

BLESSINGS OF THE PIPE

There are days where I work events outside in the summertime and it's hotter than hell, like Western desert heat, deep desert where the prehistoric thunderbirds hide! The weather patterns for Southern California shifted say over the last five years to where both the hot/cold are more noticeable now instead of gradual, no longer the eye-to-the-sky mystery it once was. It's more like Nevada in the summer and Seattle/Pacific Coast in the fall and winter. Gone are the days and nights of expected perfection in temperature during seasonal changeover, when it has a harder time deciding which way it's going to turn.

Nestled in the mountains up off Kanan Road on Mulholland Highway in Malibu is the Saddlerock Winery & Ranch, part of Malibu Family Wines, that grows 60,000 vines on 65 acres, producing six different reds, four different whites, a rose, a port and a sparkling wine. It also doubles as a venue for weddings and events, with four different settings; The Garden, The Oakgrove, Camp Cabernet, and The Vineyard, a quaint octagonal stone house called Chateau Le Dome, located on a hillside overlooking the vines and the property overall ,to accommodate guest counts from 50 to 2000. The ranch complete with horses, zebras and where the buffalo roam is quite a beautiful site, facilitating many parties and gatherings of all kinds.

I love the place, but working there in the heart of the summer is a different story. There's only parking down below in the lot and you have to be shuttled up to the hilltop. It's always a bitch for me in particular because my bar kit of preferred and comfortable necessities is so much that it takes two trips to complete, as opposed to just driving my truck up for the drop off and then park back down below and take the shuttle back up empty-handed. Either way, it all takes extra time and effort, so arriving on-location earlier than my scheduled call time is a must, and with it being scorching out doesn't help matters when you've already broken a sweat before you even start setting up the bar.

I lived in Arizona for many years where you get used to a certain degree of high temps, but working in it is different than just lounging or playing in it, where you can go in and out taking breaks. I think I've slowly been spoiled with weather more to my liking since moving to California in 1985, therefore decreasing my interest in being out under the blazing sun for hours on end. Outside on the job from June through September, I'm always longing for dusk if it's an early afternoon start.

It's gorgeous up there no doubt, but the grounds surrounding the geometric house on the hill are a bit uneven in several areas, so staging the wedding and reception in regards to placement of the tables, the bar, the dance floor and the DJ vs. confirmed guest count is important so it all looks nice and is spread out properly to fit everyone. And there's always a photographer and/or videographer at weddings, so it's important that any hung lighting for the night is attractive and nuanced with a wattage of bulbs that doesn't make it too bright or too dim, for them, the guests and for us who are working the event. This is why I always have my Velcro-adjustable finger lights with me, so if the bar has some dark areas I can happily make up for the loss and make cocktails with them on, of which the guests get a big kick out of, as they've never seen them before. I can see their minds spinning with the ideas of their use.

The maximum you can have up there comfortably is no more than 100 people. This gig that happened in the summer of 2008, we had about 75 guests, which in my opinion is even better. Anymore and it stars getting a bit tight. With catering, you're bringing the food and kitchen line set-up as well, that's on the other side of the house, so every department has its own *mise-en-place*. Some of the bar product, red wine especially, had to be kept in the unused kitchen area in the house to keep cool. The 50lb. ice bags are in the long igloos, but it still melts as if they were laid up against a tree. It's like any situation, you just do what you can and hope for the best.

At the end of my set-up, I'm soaked, so I shuttle down to the truck to take a breather, towel myself off, change clothes and have a smoke before , yet once again, go back up in the shuttle. I get back behind the bar and do some final rearranging of tools, tubs and expanded product chilling while shape-shifting my mood for customer service with me alive and kicking, more close-up and personal than real bar establishments. There's less technicality and management oversight with it, more loose and fun with the only camera on me being the eyes of the guests.

So I'm hanging out and ready to rock with guests arriving shortly, and I see this guy with really long hair walking with a woman in the distance, slowly getting closer and closer. My sunglasses are on, so no one can see exactly where I'm looking, just a general direction. And low and behold, I knew who they were, the last people I expected to see there, my sweat lodge leaders, Wolf and Lisa Wahpepah. We greeted, as it had been a year or so since the Malibu sweat lodge on old Piuma Road up on the property of the architect, Frank Lloyd Wright, had closed due to new fire hazard code. This was an amazing property at the top overlooking the Pacific Ocean.

This lodge happened on Monday evenings, a perfect day off to participate in the Native American Indian ceremony of purification, the first stage of the Red Road/Sundance experience, of which I did once or twice a month for a couple years. It was great to see them, but I was surprised as to why they were there, aside from them potentially being invited guests of the bride and groom. They were licensed to officiate the wedding and perform the marriage ceremonies. Who would've thought? I had no idea they did this on the side. All the sudden I felt like I was back with my tribe. If the bride and groom hired them, they must be doing sweats too. A comfort came over me and I was set for the night.

Guests poured in by shuttle drops, so my activity making drinks and serving wine and beer was occurring in rushes and waves. It was warm, so I knew what was going to happen, a quenching of the thirst for an hour until everyone was present, and then the announcement of the ceremony about to begin, which took place down at the end of a forty-yard narrow, overgrown path that opened up to a flat lawn space for seating, where the vows are exchanged beneath a fallen oak tree arch entwined with grapevines, a very cool setting to be one with nature.

Wolf and Lisa even performed the pipe ceremony in the middle of the service. The bowl is made of a red stone called pipestone, and the stem is made of wood. The bowl, the female part, from mother earth, receives the stem, the male part. With this unity, it becomes very strong medicine. Lisa begins the pipe-loading song, and the pipe is loaded with red willow bark and prayers. The prayers are said to the seven directions; East, South, West, North, Below, Within and Above. If the bride and groom wish to smoke from the pipe, they take one puff without drawing the smoke into the lungs, then they gently blow out so the smoke sends the prayers to the wind and the spirits, and that completes the connection, as the prayers are spoken by Wolf.

The ceremony lasts about 30-40 minutes. I took a breather to regroup my bar needs and stock up to start fresh again for the reception. I have glassware for the adults and plastic cups for the kids. I serve everyone. I dig making Shirley Temples for the young ones just so I can see the look in their eyes. It's a treat for them. They love being able to belly up to the bar at an outdoor event like a grownup. Once they realize that I'm basically a kid at heart too, then they relax their initial apprehension when ordering sodas and juices. I'll even make them special no-alcohol concoctions if I have the right stuff of selection to play with. The adults have cocktails, the kids have mocktails. I aim to please!

As the ceremony ends, the waiters are ready with their trays of appetizers to pass as the guests walk back up to the main area. And here I go again, getting busy with some serious cocktailing, slowly hit by everyone this time. It's always a challenge to go in and out of high gear for hours. But I'm used to it after thousands of events to keep the energy rolling at the bar, the fun spot to hang out, with my position being the first direct and reoccurring contact point with the people. I have to be on my best, cheerful behavior at all times.

The DJ starts the musical engine for everyone to catch a groove of enjoyment, while Wolf and Lisa make it up to the bar for a spirited libation after a glass of water or lemonade at the spigot jar self-serve station. It was nice to see them in a different setting where they weren't conducting the lodge gatherings or anything, where they had a seat at a table like every other guest. And for them to see me do what I do was probably a bit strange for them as well, in and out of each other's elements. But hey, after a couple drinks, who cares?

It turned out to be a beautiful evening once the sun set over the highest peak in the distance, and the lights turning into a night party, with the blessing of a mild, cool breeze crossing bodies in silent relief. Dinner was served at its scheduled timing following the post-ceremony reception of about ninety minutes. The DJ took over as Emcee during the last half of dining for the usual activity of giving the microphone over to the parents of the bride and groom, and eventually anyone else in the crowd of family and friends who wanted to say a few words to the new couple.

Meanwhile, I'm hanging out behind the bar trying to stay busy and occupied with whatever, though I sometimes will take a bottle of red and white with me and go around to the tables, mostly at

Pierre's request, even though there are bottles already on the table, it just feels nice to go out and mingle a stretch, and then disappear, like I've never been gone! My work is my favorite energy mode to be in, which is probably why I still like to do the job to this day. Making drinks for people and talking with them is fun, no stress, I've learned to take it all in stride.

Following some after-dinner relaxation with walking around, the guests are ready to party, and the DJ kicks up the dance floor with some great music from the 60's to 90's mainly, very fitting for the crowd, and myself. I'm busy again with more drinks, but a steadier pace this time with no hurry of thirst.

There's a point in any private gig that I do where dinner is served, like this wedding for example, where at the beginning I'm buried during the initial bar set-up and then the reception hits the bar heavy right after the ceremony, which is why I'm usually the first floor staffer to arrive and many times even the last one to leave at night. So there's a middle period during guest/table sit-down where the bar gets a short respite and slides into a cruise control when it picks back up.

This is when the floor waiters and food really gets rolling into their high-volume phase with its three courses and sometimes more, depending on if it's plated or buffet style. This lull was welcomed not only to catch up behind the bar, but to have a chance to chat with Wolf and Lisa whenever they walked up for another drink. At other venues where the grounds of the event are more spread out, I may have to switch from a bar in one area to a bar in another area, which means I have to uproot all my bar gear and schlep it over with me and lay it all out again. That's a drag!

This venue location is truly beautiful, but it's a bit trying and stressing on the mind and body in the summer heat. But all goes well with another event pulled off with excellent execution. It's funny, all the events and parties I do basically being a touring bartender all over L.A., into the thousands now, and with the bar being the number one spot that guests love to frequent and hang out at through the night, which by the way includes a lot of communication gig after gig, but when it comes to my own life, I don't even know how to go out anymore and hang on that side of the bar as a guest or customer. It's just a weird "fish out of water" feeling for me. It's hard to have much interest or care about going out or to a bar when I already spend so much time out and behind them.

I break down the bar here on the hill, gather my gear once again, get my paperwork for the next gig from the caterer and take the last shuttle down.

23

MEMORIAM

Death happens. And once or twice a year I get the call. Whether it be a burial or cremation, there are times when a memorial service or after-service gathering takes place at home. Family and friends meet in a more natural setting, the environment in which the person who passed once lived. The feeling is warmer and more relaxed.

I usually know beforehand what I'm walking into, especially with this type of get-together. I step into the home with an energy of quietude, moving slowly and looking for the person in charge, the client. This was in October of 2008 in the Bel-Air area of Los Angeles just off of Sunset Blvd., which is basically the zip code right next door to Beverly Hills.

I met the daughter who was taking care of everything, and found out later on that it was her mother, entertainer Edie Adams, who passed away. Though she was a star of stage, screen and TV, Edie was best known for her sensual delivery in pitching Muriel Cigars in ads and commercials in the 60's with her come-on line "Why don't you pick one up and smoke it sometime?"

Edie was previously married to comedian, actor and writer Ernie Kovacs, and West Coast jazz trumpeter Pete Candoli, who played with the big bands of Woody Herman, Stan Kenton, Benny

Goodman, Tommy Dorsey, Les Brown and others. He was inducted into the International Jazz Hall of Fame in 1997 along with his jazz trumpeter brother, Conte, who with his many musical credits including Dizzy Gillespie, Gerry Mulligan, Frank Sinatra and Bing Crosby, was also a member of Doc Severinsen's NBC Orchestra on The Tonight Show with Johnny Carson.

It was only a gathering of 40-50 people expected to show, so the two of us, myself on the bar and Desiree on the floor ,was all that was needed to assist in the food and beverage department. Desiree and I showed up on the street to park just about at the same time. It was a very steep incline of the road. I was one side of the street and she was on the other. We walked in together.

From what I heard, there was a service elsewhere earlier in the day, so we had a call time of 3:00pm for a 4:00pm start . This is smart timing for family and friends because it beats most of the rush hour traffic early on, and ends with people leaving around 8:00pm, back in normal traffic. Unfortunately, with L.A, it's one of those timings where it's always better to figure in for guest considerations. It was also on a weekday, which helped the ease of everything.

Nice and mellow was the play of the day for me at the bar. Not sad, nor cheery, just somewhere comfortably in the middle. At this stage of performing the work for so long, one could safely say that I've earned a masters degree in human relations (or guest relations in my case) with a minor if not double-major in psychology. No classroom studies required when you're working with humanity, the real thing gig-in and gig-out in elements outside of a closed room in an office on the 15th floor of a high-rise building. Next to bartenders as someone to talk to with discretion, people usually like to spill it to shrinks. It's easier than talking to their spouses. But the bartender position is #1. And there's a reason. Shrinks cost hundreds of dollars an hour, when bartenders simply appreciate a generous tip, with no paperwork or billing of insurance. It's just too bad I can't find a way to put the sensory overload of my eidetic memory to a better, more valuable use in terms of financially productive gain outside of the bar.

That's the one bummer with how education is set-up in this country, is that you can earn OJT (On Job Training) credits in high school when you're also working a job, but it doesn't continue on when you're out of school and in the real working world, so I can't use the decades of experience as college credits toward a degree on paper, where I could enter those occupational fields mentioned. I would have to take all the other questionably meaningless-to-the-role side courses that are always part of the scholastic mountain to climb, all in the name of rounding out the curriculum, and of course for the universities to make more money! It's much like a bill that goes to the senate floor for a vote, but by the time it finally arrives, all this other pork belly shit is added and/or hidden into the bill that doesn't really belong there.

The bar is set-up in the covered patio outside in back, near the screen door that leads into the main dining room. Perfect, outdoors, nice day, though a slight chill entered into the evening. temps. The beverage inventory delivered was filled with everything needed for a full bar, with all the basic spirits and mixers, liqueurs, juices, sodas, waters, fruit, and a nice wine and beer selection. And I can make a few classic and specialty drinks if so requested.

It's nice to not have the bar product so trim to the point where I can barely make anything mentionable. There's been a few times where that sort of thing has happened in the past when it comes to spirits and cocktails heavily minimized, making it a difficult limitation which can sometimes lead to all of it running out quickly when there's not a wider selection to please the range of people's drinking interests. If I don't have their preferred spirit and mixer, they may end up choosing just a wine or beer. But you never want the guest to have to settle for a different category of drink if you can avoid it.

As I get the bar organized and chilled down, the restaurant deli caterer drops off the variety of small munchies and desserts in large tins, for Desiree to transfer over onto some of the nicer kitchen plates, Lazy Susan turntables, and large bowls, along with condiments and silverware, and all placed attractively on the long cleared-off dining table, just eyeshot of the bar area.

My gears are always set to go with the flow, high or low. The invites of family and friends began arriving. I can see them way down on the street below the raised property, as it was to my back outside where the bar was. The home was a very cool 60's-ish dig, not as big as your typical sprawling estate for the neighborhood. Though, I'm sure it had a floor below or partial above way in back not easily noticeable from the inside. That's the thing about curious floor plans. They beckon one to explore the mystery of the layout and the history of who's lived there before.

I got busy with some drinks for guests and greetings at the bar, a few of them grabbing a smoke at the same time, while Desiree comes out to the side of the bar to grab a few cocktails for other guests inside hanging out and chatting, many of them catching up with old friends or past business associates they hadn't seen in quite a while. That sort of strange time distance between hookups can happen when you live in such a big, spread out area like Los Angeles where many seem to live so far apart from who they know, not to mention work drives. You have the San Fernando Valley, Pasadena, Downtown, over the hill in L.A. proper and Hollywood, Santa Monica on the west side, the beach areas, Malibu and the Palisades. That's a lot of territory!

With this sort of low-keyed event, I initially prefer to have the guest engage with me when at the bar instead of myself being forward with anything else beyond a hello and what can I get you to drink? If it's a comfortable place in the conversation, I can offer my condolences to them for who their loss, but it's also not the type of thing you want to end up making a habit of repeating too much either when you're in my position. In these cases, less is usually better, light and easy. However, I also don't want to come across morose all through the evening. Again, it's finding the balance of how best to communicate in any situation, given the combination of event, mood and personalities attending. There were a few kids in the mix of adults who came to the bar and ordered Shirley Temples. There are many times when I'm behind the bar almost anywhere I work and at times don't realize that I have audible sound effects going on when making drinks until someone notices. The children start to laugh and get a kick out of it, like being mesmerized by a magician with movement and creation. It's a nice accidental way to keep their spirits up.

Desiree and I were only there for five hours total. It was a short and sweet get-together of individuals both mourning their loss and celebrating the life of their dear departed friend. And I kind of feel the emotion of it when I'm there too. It can't help but permeate a little when it's all around you. It certainly makes you think about your own life and the ones you love a little deeper in that moment in time.

It got dark out soon enough, and the patio lights were turned on, keeping some shine on the bar to the degree I prefer, without it being so bright where I would have to put sunglasses on. There's nothing worse than a badly lit bar. It has to be just right to produce a certain visual look and appeal both close up and from a distance. With Desiree coming out to the bar for more drinks, my work was a pretty easy cruise to just stay put behind the bar and keep company with those who were outside talking close by.

This was one of those gigs where even though it wasn't a high-energy event, the time moved by fairly quick mainly due in knowing that we weren't going to be there a sixth or seventh hour, which is the norm most of the time. I love these short gigs though. You're in and out in a snap. And it's great for Desiree too, as she has another job modeling with her identical twin sister. Sometimes, the easier the gig, the better!

Guests started to fade little by little after hanging out for a few hours. I began trimming the sails of the bar in a way where no one quite notices, and Desiree was inside doing a slow wrap and clean-down. Her and I, like others that I work with, get a feel for when we need to hit our end time on the hour. We went through some product at the bar, enough to the point where there was only a couple boxes full of still-sealed goods left for the beverage service to pick-up the next day for client reimbursement.

Edie's daughter came outside to settle up with us soon after the last guest had left. Everything went well as expected, no glitches and nothing broken! I grabbed my bar kit and off we went, back into the city at night.

24

BONUS STORY

SILO

NOTE – This is not a Bar story. This is a short story based from my childhood growing up on my Grandparent's dairy farm in upstate New York before I moved out West at the age of seven. Just wanted you to know in case you would prefer to skip this story. I put it here as a place to house it for any family and friends that wish to read and have access to it at all times.

It was the early evening, with barely a shed of daylight remaining before the night falls complete. My grandfather stood with the help of his canes in the bedroom of the small house that was built on the land just down the road from the main farm house where he and my grandmother lived in semi-retirement. Watching through the window, there was nothing that could be done. It was too late. Flames were growing tall to the sky, with the fire trucks arriving nearby.

Storrs Road runs all the way down to the water. Though cottages line the edge areas of the great Lake Ontario, the interior is soil-rich land for farming. Maybe a bit too rich in the thoughts of some, but who could complain in that direction when everything is green with envy. Ontario is derived from the Iroquois Indian word *Kanadario*, meaning "sparkling waters" or "beautiful lake". In the southern part of upstate New York, the lake is five times larger than France, covering over 400,000 square miles. I grew up here in historic Sackets Harbor until the age of seven on my grandparent's dairy farm. It is one of New York state's heritage areas and was a shipbuilding center during the War of 1812. Watertown, Dexter, Brownville, Alexandria Bay, Cape Vincent, and the St. Lawrence River are here in the Thousand Islands region within an hour or so away.

In the 1800's, my great-great grandparents migrated from a town in France called Rosiere, to Northern New York in Jefferson County, an area upstate previously settled by countrymen who came over earlier and purchased a half million acres in large tracts of land, founding the village and calling it Rosiere, near Depauville. Many of the Bonapartists driven from France came to America and settled here. Some of my descendents were soldiers in Napoleon's army.

Since my grandfather also drove the school bus in the morning and afternoon, not only did he pick me up to go to school, it made it convenient to have me dropped off at the Blackwell's house after school with their kids of my age, just a couple houses down the road from the farm, until my parents got home from work. I was the first grandchild on my father's side, so everyone always kept an eye or two on me. This was wide open land for the most part, so there's no telling where I'd roam. Even Tippy, the German shepherd farm dog made sure I didn't get too close to the main road. We had a handshake agreement !

This was the early 60's, and as a child my favorite music to listen and dance to were the Beatles. I even had a pair of Beatle boots. Through manure and mud puddles it didn't stop me from wearing them anywhere. I sang better with them on. Well, boots and M & M's !

Out of the eight children my grandparents had, five were boys and three were girls. The perfect combination for a farm, some would say. My father was the first of eight, therefore the first son to work the farm with my grandfather, then Larry and Donnie. My uncle's Charlie and Philip maintained the 12-hour work days for the most part while I was growing up, as the cows have to be milked twice a day – 5:00 am and 5:00 pm. Charlie had a more quiet but funny personality, while Philip was both funny and chatty. Gramps still liked to do his share of the work, making sure the boys didn't fall behind. Even with the damage to his legs from polio, he would still make his way up to the seat of the tractor and get some work done. At that age, I didn't know or understand why, but it didn't matter to me.

With Larry, Carolyn, and Donnie living off the res, Phyllis and Kathy remained in the farm's five-bedroom main house with Charlie, Philip, and Grandma and Grandpa. Phyllis and Philip were twins, and the youngest Kathy living upstairs in what became known as the haunted room. Many years later when she moved to the small house, she said the ghost followed her there. Maybe Kathy was the only friend it had.

With corn and oats to be cut and hay to be baled, you have seeding, cultivating and feeding that takes place in never-ending cycles. There's nothing quite like the pungency when the manure wagon is full and needs to be taken out to re-fertilize the land where the cows graze. After the boys have finished the morning milking, the bovines are released out of the barn so the electric gutter rake can go through its cleanup motions. The center walking breezeway had to be swept too, as the rakes are moving. A farm is a ranch, just with different livestock. And tending to it takes just as long a day. Gramps would back the Allis-Chalmers up to the wagon in the barn's only side garage. At one time, there was also a Farmall and Massey-Ferguson tractors in the shed.

Hooking it up with the linchpin, he would slowly head toward the main road, passing the mobile home that I lived in with my parents across from the farmhouse with the dirt road in between. I could tell it was Gramps in the seat of the tractor without looking out the window, as opposed to it being Philip or Charlie. Listening, I could hear the way each of them used the throttle and gears. That's how I told them apart. I wasn't allowed to ride with them until I was four or five years old, because of the obvious fear of falling and getting hurt. There wasn't any place to sit, so I had to jump up and stand on the rear axle, holding onto the fender handle for dear life. I was the only child in many ways, but it didn't stop me from wanting to go for it.

I was ill a lot during those years. With asthma, hay fever, bronchitis, tonsillitis, pneumonia, wheezing, and being in an oxygen tent every year, I barely had time to breathe. I also had what seemed to be endless hallucinations, scaring me out of my wits, afraid to close my eyes, where things appeared larger than life. Buildings and trees turned into moving monsters that walked and followed me. Maybe they were fever dreams, I don't know, but something took me over for a while in my ills, like a child possessed. It is the reason we eventually moved out West to Yuma, Arizona. The hot, dry heat cleaned me out, saved my life, and I grew out of the asthma.

Feeling better, I wanted to get out and do something, anything. Mom would open the door to the trailer in perfect timing when the tractor and wagon would be right there. So I'd look out into Grandpa's eyes wondering if I could go with him as he went out to spread the field. Sometimes he was in a good mood and at other times he wasn't, but he always caught my eye with that "Please get me outta here, I wanna go with you" look on my face. When he smiled, my heart lit up like the sun, then he nodded with a wave and that was my signal to run over and climb up, as he took it out of gear and helped me up with his big hands. Standing next to him sitting and steering, I was on top of the world. When we got out in the field it was a little bumpy, so I really had to hold on.

Yet the times he didn't smile or pay attention when I was there, I didn't know what to think. I didn't know what serious meant, and when he said "no . . . not today little Kyle . . . okay?", I was crushed inside, like all my energy was taken away. Mom tried to make it better, but watching him drive off without me next to him brought tears to my eyes that seemed to last forever, wondering and scared that he didn't like me anymore. Hours later, I would heal after a nap and at the scent in the air of Grandma baking toll house cookies in the main house across the way. I would wait and watch through the screen door like a CSI: Cookie Scene Investigator. She hid them because she knew I was on the lookout. They were for my uncles, not me! Then the thief of chocolate would pounce in for a couple warm ones when she left the room, and disappear.

On Fridays she would make and bake pizza from scratch for everyone. Imagine the smell of that in the fresh country air. I was in pepperoni heaven. They were cut into squares, the dimension of the big pans themselves. Grandma Branche was the backbone of the family. I remember fetching water from the well outside many times for her. My arms pumping away with kid frenzy, but taught to not overdo it to a run-over, avoiding the waste of even a drop. It took some practice, but I was never a failure at trying. Now I make those same cookies at home today, remembering.

As a child running wild on a working farm, you become the master of scents and sounds. Some good and others not so good. It becomes you, and after awhile, you get to understand the worst of them as nothing more than tones of the earth, however they may test one's senses. Like anything, you get used to it. I had a strange enjoyment from smelling Phillip and Charlie's suspender overalls, as they encompassed everything on the farm. A mixture of bright and dark, light and heavy. So I got suspenders too! In the Wintertime, the scents were less pungent in the air.

The corn fields were bare nearby and directly in back of the house. With the sun bright and the snow shimmering, a bunch of us Branche, Blackwell, and Liptrot kids who lived up and down the road would get together in the mid-mornings with a couple of snow sleds or the engine hood of a car and slide down and up the rows, all bundled up in jackets and thick pants, laughing and yelling, with freezing faces.

In the mid-afternoon I'd have to get home and cleanup when Grandpa came in from the fields, as he liked to take me with him to the American Legion in town on Main Street, and introduce me as his first grandson to all his friends. I didn't understand really. All I knew was that I got to have orange sodas and play shuffleboard for a time, touching buttons on the jukebox, and having fun hanging out with the old guys while Gramps knocked back a few. I loved the sound of the door's buzzer when you pressed the button to get in with the sound of the lock-snap following. He got happy and sang a lot on the way home, just a short distance . He had a big, deep voice. I sang along a little bit, but I really didn't know the words.

At that age, the animals were intimidating to me. Their big bodies and my little body equaled fear. Cows are mild and gentle, and don't like to be bothered by humans. You can't pet a cow for the most part. They don't quite respond like a domesticated animal, and they don't like being surprised. Watching the Holsteins come in from the field like a swaggering milk gang, slowly entering the opening of the barn doors, their hooves go from touching the brown earth to the flat concrete foundation of the barn's floor. Quick adjustments are necessary to avoid any slip and falls, so they have to move even slower and with more body weight control to walk safely in their individual stalls.

These four-legged have a humble brilliance to them. Every time, they will go into their exact same stalls, just knowing. The ultimate creatures of habit. Once in a while, one or two will get confused, but they soon figure it out on their own. The perfect feed awaits them, so locked in they go, happy with the trade. Each has their own pressure-controlled water bowls at about neck height, so for a few hours they'd hang out side-by-side with the radio on the country music station, swinging and swaying. Charlie would do the South side and Philip the North, setting up to milk them one after the other in overlapping fashion, all the way down the long stretch of the barn. They wouldn't allow me to milk the cows early on, because they were afraid I might get crushed in between two bellies that swayed too close together at the wrong time.

I used to love watching the cows after they've finished grubbing. Their jaws never stop moving, like they're always chewing something. In the early days it was manual milking, but later on an electric milking system was installed which dramatically reduced all that hands-on labor, and was cleaner and safer. All of the fresh milk was vacuum-pumped to a large main holding tank in another room connected to the barn's North side, so the big dairy truck could come by a couple times a week for pick-up. It was cooled, and I would open up the hatch at the top, watch it swirl around and smell the freshness. So much milk in one stainless steel container. Like an ocean.

On one particular visit, a calf was being born in the early morning. I swear it was the day after I arrived from Arizona. I was in bed upstairs but there was a floor vent that went from my feet down to the kitchen, so I could overhear all the talk at the table. I rose up, got dressed and went downstairs. The mother had stayed inside the barn the previous night to keep warm. I walked in the barn and Charlie and Philip were already there close by while she was laying on the floor in some degree of labor. I was about twenty feet away. The doctor was on the way over. All went well and the calf was placed on safer dirt ground with some fresh hay for better stability when on its feet.

Other times when I've watched doctors come in for health maintenance or when a cow is ill, the medicine tablets they use are huge compared to the aspirin that people take. It had to be three inches across, a perfect fit in the palm of your hand, for a reason! But it helps the livestock get better, and that's important, so it doesn't spread to others.

You don't have to live on a farm for twenty years to have it permeate in your blood for good. When I would visit every few summers, Philip and Charlie no longer had to fear the new two-legged creature popping out from nowhere as they once did when I was a little toddler. I had grown up a bit and was finally healthy for the first time, in their eyes. Now all they had to do was pray that I wouldn't nosedive the motorcycle into a nearby ditch off the side of the road. When they thought I was having too much fun, they'd pull back the reigns and make me do some honest work to earn my keep. I wanted to help, so even that was alright. Gramps and them taught me how to drive the tractor so I could help them bring wagon loads of hay in from the fields, and one by one up the conveyer belt to the barn's loft where Charlie was stacking and laying on the other end. A bit of heavy lifting for my size, I still put the gloves on and pulled my weight so they could rely on me. Can't be a lazy wimp on a farm!

One thing I had to make sure of was to never lose the linchpin. I was always aware of the little things, though. My father mentioned to me that knotholes in the wood walls at the top half of the barn have to be watched out for so direct sunbeams through them for extended periods of time wouldn't cause a bale of hay to catch fire up in the loft. Best if they're closed up. Back in the field, Gramps would reverse the tractor and combine to an empty hay wagon that I had just brought back and unhooked. I'd be standing between them both, with the pin in one hand and the connector hitch in the other, and when the holes lined up I'd shove the pin down, hooking it up to continue baling in another full load.

Summer's almost gone. The crops are finishing in, and the last wagon of hay from the just-cut field ends up being our neighborly hay ride for all family and friends nearby the old road.

Humidity hits August off the lake, sunset filled with gnats in the air at dusk, and fireflies at night. Not the best time to take a long walk, much less a bike ride without goggles and a nose-mouth piece on. Flying back from Arizona to New York as a teenager, I was hoping the Honda 70 was up and running so I could make across the countryside, through some woods and down to the cottages near the water's edge. Putting mileage on the little hummer was no problem. The wind blowing my shoulder-length hair, I was free and it was heaven to me. Charlie and Gramps had fully maintenance done from the repairman up at the top of the road, knowing I was about to arrive at the airport in Syracuse.

I was always excited to get back to what I thought was my home away from home. I walked over to see the Blackwell's and the Liptrot's just up the road a few houses, as they all knew me when I was young taking the bus to school with everyone else. As I would grow and change over the years combined with the infrequency of seeing them, they would always hesitate for a moment before they figured out who it was knocking on the screen door. A shadow memory of the past. A chameleon of continued growth. No, it's just Kyle. "How ya doin kid, we was wondering who that was riding Charlie's motorbike!".

The time would always pass by too fast during my visit. I never wanted to leave. I remember after a couple weeks, only four or five days left before I'd have to head back to the West coast. With fleeting time eating at me little by little, my one wish would not have been for a million dollars. It would've been for the clock to stop ticking away those moments I thought belonged to me. It's probably the reason why I never owned or wore a wrist watch until the age of twenty six. I wanted no reminders of time. The moving of the sun and the moon was plenty enough.

Knowing how much you're going to miss something can be a bit troubling for a teenager. Emotions and short-fused youth aggression can take over. I was wild in my mind but not a problem-causer by nature. One late afternoon a dark wind must have blew over my shoulders. I was out in the oat field with Gramps, Philip and Charlie, and one of the tractors broke down. Philip asked me to walk back to the farm and drive the other Allis-Chalmers over. It was a bit of a hike, but it's not like the main property was out of visibility. I just had to do an end-around on foot, but I ran most of the way instead. Gramps had the John Deere 4010 diesel there, but we didn't want him to have to do a round-trip and a half. And besides, the big green machine was still new, so he wasn't easy about letting anyone else drive it just quite yet.

Driving back to the field, something was bothering me. I don't know what it was. I had to give Charlie a ride back to the machinery shed to grab the tools he needed for repair. They wanted to get it done before dusk fell upon us, so I got the tractor rolling – a little too much. Charlie was standing on the hitch behind me while holding onto the seatback with one hand and the left-rear fender handle with the other. After clearing the just-cut oat field, I started through the dirt road that lead between the long stretch of corn rows on the way to the single-lane main Storrs road. It was bumpy due to the wet and dry weather changes, some potholes and well, the nature of the soil. I had the throttle up a little too high and before I knew it, Charlie was yelling for me to slow it down. As I was at the point of doing so he bounced off the back end and onto the ground. He was standing up and not hurt. I had stopped and he caught up. It was the first time something like that happened. "Get off there, let me drive", he said. Now I was in his position, holding on back the rest of the way over.

Lessons have to be taught fast on a farm, good or bad. There's no time to fart around, and it can be dangerous when not paying attention. It was my turn to learn one, but otherwise I abided well with mostly everything. He dropped me off at the main house, and that was the end of my day of helping out. One day I tried climbing one of the silos, but the cables got too far apart on the way up and my legs and arms wouldn't stretch out any more. Just as well. I didn't need an accident !

I remember the first couple of times going back to vacation for the summer. Playing Rock 'em Sock 'em Robots with Uncle Phil. Tagging along with the guys while we drove to the village of Adams to go to the machinery store for parts or whatever. I'd walk in and head right for the big wall case that held all of the kid-sized scaled replicas of the tractors and wagons we had on the farm. I could stand there and stare through the sliding glass doors for an hour. Gramps had already bought me a couple pieces that I had at home, but it wouldn't stop me from seeing if there was anything new. Then we went to Carol's Drive-In for a burger, fries and a shake before we headed back.

Visiting when I was thirteen or so, a horse was corralled in the lot just across from the farmhouse and a little ways from the barn. The owner was a friend of my grandfather, who was out of town for a few weeks. My uncles were very busy and so within a couple of hours of arriving, I was made responsible for feeding and taking care of this red Arabian stallion. He was unbroken and a bit wild. A perfect fit. After a short time, we knew how to work each other pretty well.

He had plenty of graze grass in the field, so I took care of his grains, water, and an apple every other day kept the doctor away from both of us. I could tell he wasn't too keen on sharing the sweets, so I only took a bite and let him have the rest. I would go off and do something else for a little while, then come back and jump inside the large lot and walk him around the entire field. However, the walk turned into a trot and then turned into a gallop the more I got going into a run. I eventually had to get out of the way. Catching my breath, we'd start walking and do it again and again so he'd get some exercise. Back at the front gate, I'd try to get his body close to the wood railing where I'd be sitting on top so I could slowly throw my leg over him, but he would not come over close enough for me to make the move safely. It would've been a bareback attempt, but I really wasn't interested in the worst-case scenario had he not responded well.

Just a few days after, I was in town for part of the day to find out when I got back that a few older guys from around the area had just tried to ride him. That pissed me. But after the first one got bucked off from what I was told, it pretty much closed up the idea of any further tries, even saddled up. I guess my instincts were right, but him and I were buddies so I probably wouldn't have received the same rude awakening as the neighborhood fella's did. Good horse sense !

On some evenings I'd be over at the Blackwell's house visiting, as Flora had four children that I grew up with, including Mark who was my age. It was fun to catch up with everyone. When I'd head back to the house, it was so pitch dark out with no streetlights, I couldn't see the road directly in front of me, even after my eyes attempted to adjust. All I could see at a distance on the right was the porch light, far away. Talk about fright nights! I started jogging silently so I could get there quicker since my heart was beating out of my chest anyway!

Closer, and slowly in my vision I could see the fireflies hovering around the bulb gathering some heat. When they were younger, my mother and my Aunt Billie used to call them lightning bugs. I remember visiting after I graduated high school when I was seventeen. My parents had bought me plane tickets as a graduation gift. Philip and his wife, Melanie, had now been living in the main house on the farm for several years now by themselves, so I stayed with them. Charlie was living up the road. Weeks went by too quickly even for a laid-back pace of lifestyle, and again, it was time for me to go.

Grandma and Gramps would always drive me back to the airport in Syracuse. It was another early morning take-off, I guess in order to get into Arizona at a decent hour, with the mid-country layover in Chicago. It was about a seventy-mile drive, and I was sitting in the back seat alone. I could overhear my grandparents talking about things. I wasn't paying attention much, as I was staring out the window in my own little world. They'd ask me something now and then or I'd do the same. As we entered into the passenger drop-off area of the airport, the car came to a stop. Gramps turned off the motor, while Grandma went in to see if my plane was going to be taking off on time.

Within a few moments of silence, something hit me. They were getting a little older, and I guess I was too. I didn't know when I would be back again, and that kind of scared me. After a little bit of last minute talking via the rearview mirror, Gramps turned around and I moved up to the middle of the back seat. We looked at each other and started crying, missing one another already. A couple times during my stay, we had sat in the living room and watched a baseball or football game together. I could smell the cherry tobacco in his pipe. I was this kid, strong-willed, but couldn't hold it together when it came to things like this; missing people, not knowing when I'd see them again.

Grandma arrived back to the car. Everything was running on schedule. I was hoping it would be late. It was difficult for Gramps to get out of the car and walk through the airport, so we hugged and kissed goodbye. Grandma went back in with me. It was the last time I saw my grandfather. We both had that feeling but couldn't put it into words, and didn't want to. At a certain checkpoint I had to go on my own. I hugged and kissed my grandmother goodbye, and told her that I loved her and I'll see you soon. Even though I had a special bond with both of them, she knew I had a special connection with Gramps.

I remember him getting on me about making a groove path in the lawn above the ditch off the side of the road with the motorcycle, creating a fun jump for myself, but he didn't care too much for what it was doing to the grass. I was being a bit thoughtless so, I would say "okay" and that would be the end of it. I stopped riding up it. No endless harps about it as long as I did what I was told. I got the message.

Here I was, roaming through the airport trying to find my gate with still-streaming tears in my eyes. I must've looked like a lost kid, but I was used to finding my own way through terminals. I just had to clear my eyes and find a bathroom to blow my nose.

Some years had gone by and I was going through a lot of changes in my life, working at a regular job now and paying rent like everyone else. I hardly had any monies leftover for play or vacation. I was working many hours and two jobs, living in Phoenix when the call came in a couple days after the fact.

It happened around 7:00 pm, October 5th, 1981.

It was fairly calm outside. Some days of wind and rain had hit a month and two before, when the hay is cut and baled up into the barn's loft in August and September. Turning dark quickly, Philip and Charlie were a little more than half the way through with milking the cows for the evening, when Phil noticed the lights flickering in the barn. This triggered a sign of two possibilities; electrical or temperature. There were three silos on the South side of the barn, right up next to it. The opposite side of where the main house was. It continued, so he took a further walk around and then went out back. Near the silo side, that's where he noticed it.

Fire and smoke was coming from a corner of the barn loft. Phil immediately ran into the barn yelling to let Charlie know and to call the fire department. The main priority at that moment was to get the cows out of the barn, so one-by-one they were released from their stalls after the milking apparatus was moved off the floor and out of the way of the four cows currently being milked, two on each side. Not a moment to waste, the problem of containment had begun from the first notice of the flames, as the loft was full of hay just above.

The power to the barn's lighting had to be shut off from the main power box, as the hot wiring above is what caused the flickering below. Dark inside, the cows were backing up trying to move onto the center breezeway and find their direction out the side barn door, slowing things up. A flashlight quickly helped show the way. Spreading fast above, smoke was moving everywhere. By the time they finally got all the cows out, the fire trucks arrived and needed to clear the area inside and out. The roof was soon to be engulfed.

Not able to get over there in time to rescue them out of their separated pens, two calves died in the barn. This was a country fire. No pale of water was going to help reduce it any. Even with an entire lake so close, nothing could be done. It was high in the sky for almost seven hours. What all of the neighbors on old Storrs Road grew up with all those years as children and adults, and people that babysat me when I was young, watched through the trees of the road in tears as a family and area landmark in a small historic town, burned away.

It was spontaneous combustion. There was some wet/damp hay up in the loft, with some dry hay sitting on top of it. It started to sweat, and eventual heat levels rose to the point where it caught fire.

A quarter-mile down the land stretch on the road in a smaller retirement house built, my grandparents looking North out of their bedroom window, could only stand and stare at the decades of work possibly coming to an end. With a strong will and strong hands, it was a helpless situation. All the relatives living nearby had been contacted and drove over as soon as they could get there. But the way of life of a farming family had come to a screeching halt, and no one knew what to do or think for a while after.

Thoughts and worries filled the days and weeks to come, while the cows had to be transported and milked elsewhere, not to mention grazing and feeding. Eventually the decision was made to not rebuild, for many reasons. A couple years went by and, having suffered a major heart attack, my grandfather passed away in the Jefferson County Hospital in the spring of 1984. He was 72. He tried to stay alive, but there was just too much irreversible damage. I was never able to speak to him on the phone to his hospital room. When he died, I still hadn't completely gotten over the loss the fire caused, and it's like it started all over again for me. He was one of thirteen children, with most of them still alive today, in their nineties.

Today, the silos still remain along with the main farmhouse, unoccupied. A friend of the family who has a cottage down by the edge of the lake, bought up the property and surrounding land, and has kept it virtually untouched ever since, allowing for no development or changes. After forty plus years of tilling the soil, milking cows, and supplying dairy products the last thing it deserved was a tragic ending. My grandmother survived and lived on for more than a decade. I visited her often as she stayed in town in a retirement home nearby the families.

I still go back every few years, in the summer, as the winters are too cold for me to handle, being so used to the warm weather of the West. It's beautiful at that time of year off the sparkling lake. I stay on Main Street in Sackets at a hotel off the water. After a late-morning breakfast, I borrow my Uncle Donnie's bicycle and peddle to the farm, like I always do. I'd bike from the Harbor Hotel, around and past the Madison Barracks with my first stop being the old cemetery where my grandparents are buried. I walk the bike over to the gravestone and sit on the ground for a while, and just get there for a moment. I slow it down and doze off a bit, thinking of the past, and of them. I was never really afraid in the graveyard. It was quiet.

A mile or two away is old Storrs Road, where I make a left and head up to the property, peddling faster. From a distance I could see the farmhouse and the tall silos, like pillars of power once storing and fermenting the grains and greens for all the livestock. Corn silage or fodder, as they called it. "Branche Farms" was painted close to the top of the middle silo. The closer I got the more I felt at peace. Entering the driveway, the sun was kissing the water just right. The West side of the house was receiving a long period of extra shine, warming its bones again from the most recent winter.

I sit on the porch of the vacant farm house with memories flooding my mind, like I've never left. It's warm, and I can hear the breeze telling me all is okay here. I don't have to worry anymore. I can relax. I can smile and feel a sense of deep happiness, but not without a river of tears coming on and filling my eyes. It takes a while to pass, and then I can breathe deeply in.

I wave at people I used to know, and that used to know me. We were little then, but we're still able to recognize each other just enough to say hello, and go about our day. After a while of doing nothing but staring at the hay fields being cut nearby, the sky being blue, and Ontario rocking with ski boat waves, I watch as two crows come near, landing at the top of the fireplace to join me in the sitting.

Every once in a great while I still have the dreams. Being in the farmhouse at night, being outside, standing in the barn, or walking the dark road. My grandparents would visit me, smiling to let me know that everything's alright. Then I wake up from the trance. Of all the grandchildren, I was the only one who ever lived on the farm from what I can remember. I can only wish that all of my cousins had experienced it in the same way that I did early on.

Website – www.SacketsHarborNY.com

ABOUT THE AUTHOR

Kyle Branche is a 30-year veteran professional and private bartender in Los Angeles. Originally from the historic village of Sackets Harbor, off the edge of Lake Ontario in the Southern part of upstate New York in the Thousand Islands region near Cape Vincent where he was raised on his Grandparents' dairy farm up until the age of seven. From there he moved out West to Arizona, though went back in the Summertime of his early teens to vacation and help with the farm chores of driving tractor, cutting fields, baling hay, feeding cows, and riding the farms' Honda 70 motorbike anywhere and everywhere.

While in Phoenix as a rack jobber in the music business, where he received sales display awards from Columbia Recording Artists, Journey and Willie Nelson, and then as a manager of a computer warehouse, he also moonlighted on the weekends as a barback at an establishment nearby where he lived. He then got hired at a brand new Embassy Suites Hotel, eventually transferring to Los Angeles and the bigger bar scene in 1985.

His wide variety of bartending experiences in the City of Angels is second to none, having worked in many bars, nightclubs, private clubs, restaurants, hotels, concert venues, and is currently more off the grid today working a busy, yet more flexible schedule as a private on-call bartender with a variety of services, caterers, event planners, brand-sponsored events and private clientele working the party circuit throughout the spread out metropolis. while still holding position in the bar at The Gardenia Room in Hollywood for 22 years. His Blog of stories and encounters is culled from many moons behind the bar, now in his fourth decade.

Kyle was a contributing writer and columnist in the leading beverage magazines from 2002-2012, with 75 published pieces, including the monthly cocktail column "Liquid Kitchen" with Patterson's Beverage Journal (now The Tasting Panel), feature cover stories, contributing articles, and one online multimedia super feature story on Cognac with Sante Magazine, titled "The Sleeping Spirit". Aside form creating 60+ signature cocktails, his bar line Cocktail Art Productions has produced 18 titles including seven books, two DVD's, an audio CD Book, cocktail recipe cards, calendars, and postcards.

As a culinary artist, he started his cocktail photography series in 2007. His custom Zazzle store (zazzle.com/KBranche) uses 70 drink images from this series on a variety of everyday products and specialty items, including USPS-approved Cocktail Postage Stamps, Coffee Mugs, Greeting Cards, Men's and Women's T-Shirts and Hoodies, iPod Cases, iPad Cases, iPhone cases, Mousepads, Postcards, Hats, Aprons, Necklaces, Prints and Posters, all just for a fun and creative artistic outlet. Kyle also created and designed a board game called "Cocktail Hotel."

He's also co-produced and co-hosted the cocktail shows "Liquid Kitchen" and "Beverage Road," has written a treatment for a one-hour dramatic television series titled "Life Behind Bars," played the character of "Clive, the Bartender from the Dead" in the short film "The Hounds of Bakersfield," and the part of "Lyle the Bartender" in the upcoming feature film "Frozen Tundra." Other on-camera work includes his two Cocktail Art DVD's of "live and close-up" specialty and classic drink preparations.

Made in the USA
Middletown, DE
01 June 2020